THE ECLIPSE
OF SCOTTISH CULTURE

Inferiorism and the Intellectuals

To Our Parents

Acknowledgments

Certain sections of these essays are based on articles published in *Cencrastus*, the *Bulletin of Scottish Politics*, the *Edinburgh Review*. Acknowledgment is due to the editors and publishers. These journals have kept available over the years a forum for ideas on Scottish culture uncongenial to the social and academic establishment of this country. Amongst many others, Bill Findlay, Glen Murray and Geoff Parker have at different times been particularly helpful as commentators and editors.

Finally, it is a pleasure to thank Cairns Craig, not only for his assistance as General Editor of this series, but for his intellectual generosity and stimulation over the years.

C.B.   R.T.

THE ECLIPSE
OF SCOTTISH CULTURE

Inferiorism and the Intellectuals

Craig Beveridge
and
Ronald Turnbull

Polygon
determinations⟩

© 1989 Polygon
22 George Square, Edinburgh

Typeset using the Telos Text Composition System
from Digital Publications Ltd., Edinburgh
and printed in Great Britain by
Redwood Burn Limited, Trowbridge

ISBN   0 7486 6000 3
           0 7486 6009 7 pbk

Contents

Series Preface

CAIRNS CRAIG

Scotland's history is often presented as punctuated by disasters which overwhelm the nation, break its continuity and produce a fragmented culture. Many felt that 1979, and the failure of the Devolution Referendum, represented such a disaster: that the energetic culture of the 1960s and 1970s would wither into the silence of a political waste land in which Scotland would be no more than a barely distinguishable province of the United Kingdom.

Instead, the 1980s proved to be one of the most productive and creative decades in Scotland this century—as though the energy that had failed to be harnessed by the politicians flowed into other channels. In literature, in thought, in history, creative and scholarly work went hand in hand to redraw the map of Scotland's past and realign the perspectives of its future.

In place of the few standard conceptions of Scotland's identity that had often been in the past the tokens of thought about the country's culture, a new and vigorous debate was opened up about the nature of Scottish experience, about the real social and economic structures of the nation, and about the ways in which the Scottish situation related to that of other similar cultures throughout the world.

It is from our determination to maintain a continuous forum for such debate that *Determinations* takes its title. The series will provide a context for sustained dialogue about culture and politics in Scotland, and about those international issues which directly affect Scottish experience.

Too often, in Scotland, a particular way of seeing our culture, of representing ourselves, has come to dominate our perceptions because it has gone unchallenged—worse, unexamined. The vitality of the culture should be measured by the intensity of debate which it generates rather than the security of ideas on which it rests. And should be measured by the extent to which creative, philosophical, theological, critical and political ideas confront each other.

If the determinations which shape our experience are to come from within rather than from without, they have to be explored and evaluated and acted upon. Each volume in this series will seek to be a contribution to that *self*-determination; and each volume, we trust, will require a response, contributing in turn to the on-going dynamic that is Scotland's culture.

Introduction

These essays are about cultural power, and the possibility of cultural change. On the one hand they question certain images and discourses that profoundly affect the ways in which Scots apprehend themselves and their world. These are not the only available representations of Scotland, but they are especially powerful and pervasive, and of special importance, since they function to reinforce Scotland's political subordination. Challenging these readings is therefore also a political project (just as perpetuating them can never be a matter of purely academic import).

On the other hand we attempt to recover and re-assert alternative images and discourses: ways of conceiving Scottish history and culture which do not and could not service external control, and which, for this reason, are perhaps necessarily marginalised and disqualified within our existing cultural world. The aim, in simple terms, is to analyse cultural oppression in the Scottish context, and to offer different perspectives on Scottish traditions as a basis for cultural liberation and renewal.

To interpret the central tendencies within this cultural milieu we rely on the concept of inferiorisation, which was developed by Frantz Fanon in his account of the psycho-cultural dimensions of national subordination in the Third World. Fanon argues that the native comes to internalise the message that local customs are inferior to the culture of the coloniser, a theme which runs through cultural production in the colony. In the first chapter, this model is applied to the Scottish scene and it is argued that conventional modes of reading Scottish culture — for instance the myth of Scottish inarticulacy, or the conception of Scotland's pre-Union history as an age of darkness and superstition — illustrate the adoption by Scottish intellectuals of metropolitan ways of seeing Scotland. The inferiorist reflex is also expressed in an inability to respond to Scottish practices which are not sanctioned by metropolitan culture. The fate of Scottish approaches to philosophy is viewed as a consequence of this paralysis.

We look closely at the historiographic effects, in the Scottish instance, of these attitudes to the pre-colonial past. It is argued that from the late nineteenth century onwards, a particular historical perspective has achieved increasing dominance. This perspective — which extends to each historical sphere, economic, social, cultural — is discovered to rely upon a number of assumptions and assertions which, though simple-minded, are constantly reiterated.

Crude polarities both of language and of normative historical judgement are shown to reinforce a historiographical perspective which both devalorises the pre-colonial experience and denies it any creative or formative role in post-assimilation achievement. It is emphasised that challenge to this view of the Scottish past is doubly difficult in the face of the social and cultural power within Scottish institutions of an out-posted sub-metropolitan intelligentsia.

However, in the succeeding chapter, an effort is made to trace the distortive effects of this historiography in the sphere of rural history — but also to illustrate that alternative perspectives are possible, particularly in the context of the increased confidence and capabilities of indigenous publishing houses since the nationalist revival of the seventies.

One of the most distinguished converts to the nationalist cause in the seventies was Tom Nairn, a leading figure in Britain's New Left movement, and for many, no doubt, the outstanding analyst of the Scottish predicament. Nairn's work has been seen as an important new departure in nationalist thinking, the elaboration of a nationalist position shorn of the provincialism, embarrassing sentimentality and cosy self-delusion held to be characteristic of popular nationalism. In our analysis of Nairn's nationalism in Chapter Three, we acknowledge the value of certain aspects of his work — for example his critique of the 'internationalist' position — but question whether his approach is on the whole a fruitful one from the point of view of the development of nationalist theory — and whether, indeed, it can be considered a nationalist position at all. In particular we challenge Nairn's model of Scotland's cultural development, which, it seems to us, is based on an uncritical acceptance of English readings. In this respect, Nairn's work exemplifies the peculiar potency of the 'inferiorist' code described in the first chapter, the powerful hold, even on our most sophisticated and radical thinkers, of metropolitan ideology.

Scottish education has been portrayed — in a host of poems, novels, autobiographies and scholarly studies — as reactionary and constricting, a 'grimly authoritarian and narrow' approach, to quote T.C. Smout. This perspective is so dominant that few Scots now have any appreciation of the positive features of local educational traditions. In 'Philosophical Education' we outline the recovery of local educational values in George Davie's *Democratic Intellect*, and present an account of the most powerful twentieth century re-statement of the ideal of the Scottish tradition, the educational philosophy of John Anderson, which defends, against the prevalent fashions of the age, the conception of education as humanist, theoretical and critical.

English intellectual life is expressed in and moulded by a specialist and empiricist philosophical tradition; the establishment of the English approach to philosophical studies in Scottish universities is therefore a significant modality of English cultural power. 'Philosophy and Autonomy' argues the importance of the question of philosophy (an issue which until now has been largely neglected by cultural nationalists). After analysing the main features of modern British philosophy, we describe the resistance among Scottish thinkers to the triumph of the analytic regime, and the continuing commitment to an alternative philosophical style.

Finally, we offer a brief account of the vitality of recent Scottish theory, as witnessed in the contributions of figures such as Anderson, John Macmurray, Alasdair MacIntyre and R.D. Laing. This section is no substitute for the detailed and comprehensive treatments of modern Scottish thought which are required, and which our universities are failing so signally to provide; but perhaps enough is done here to indicate an alternative to the 'black hole' view of modern Scottish culture — the notion that, after the Enlightenment, Scotland ceased to produce important thinkers. The inferiorist view is as false as it is powerful.

1

Inferiorism

The nationalist movement which shook Scotland out of its torpor in the sixties and seventies was overwhelmingly practical in character, a nationalism which lacked a substantial cultural and philosophical component. This fact was noted by many observers — the standard comparison was with nationalism in Wales — but it was not, at the time, adequately evaluated.

What cultural debate there was seemed cast in pre-war moulds, a situation symbolised by the preoccupation with MacDiarmid and by discussion about the suitability of Scots as a literary medium (a re-run of the Muir-MacDiarmid dispute). Most political thinking had a similarly antique aura (Macleanism for example). The SNP's advance at the electoral level was not matched by any corresponding intellectual achievement.

Missing, as a result, were a comprehensive account of the cultural effects of the Union, a developed awareness of the character of Scottish cultural traditions and a convincing programme for cultural change. In education, nationalists might call for more local control of our schools and universities, but they failed to project the conception of the distinctiveness of Scottish approaches to education which alone could properly have legitimated their demands. Orthodox ways of reading Scottish culture and history — those sanctioned by the academic establishment and the British media — went largely unchallenged. This problem was not addressed by appeals for the reform of abuses like the neglect of Scottish literature and history in our educational institutions. Suspicious of concepts like 'tradition' and 'identity', many tough-minded left-wing nationalists were even prepared to abandon the cultural argument entirely. Scottish nationalism's cultural-intellectual base was therefore altogether too narrow for the nationalist challenge to be sustained over any extended period.

The channelling of energies into theoretical activity which has occurred since 1979 is not so much an expression of despair over political defeat as an indication that the need for greater sophistication at the theoretical level, as a condition of further and lasting political success, is now being recognised.

A more adequate nationalist philosophy must come to terms with the pervasive effects of Scotland's dependency in relation to England. The linguistic-literary consequences of the Union, the main concern of the inter-war figures, have been much discussed, but the impact on other areas of Scottish culture, and on the total cultural milieu, has not yet been properly explored. At the same time, little use has been made, to illuminate the Scottish predicament, of work on other instances of cultural subordination. This essay attempts to indicate how these defects could be remedied: drawing on a central concept in the work of Frantz Fanon, we sketch a general model for the interpretation of Scotland's cultural condition.

I

The concept of inferiorisation, developed by Fanon in his account of the strategies and effects of external control in the Third World, seems to us to yield valuable insights and perspectives on the Scottish predicament. Fanon uses the idea to describe those processes in a relationship of national dependence which lead the native to doubt the worth and significance of inherited ways of life and embrace the styles and values of the coloniser. These processes are not to be seen as 'merely superstructural'; it is through the undermining of the native's self-belief and the disintegration of local identity that political control is secured.

According to Fanon, a colonised people is subjected to a process of mystification. Central to this process is a sustained belittling of the colonised culture, which is depicted, by the coloniser, as impoverished, backward, inferior, primitive. Fanon writes: 'Every effort is made to bring the colonised person to admit the inferiority of his culture. . .'[1]

Science and scholarship contribute to this undertaking, as in the work of the French psychiatrists Fanon quotes who tried to demonstrate that African 'primitivism' was due to physical features of the brain.

Another theme in colonialist ideology is the native's barbarism. In pre-colonial times, it is asserted, the natives lived in savagery, and it is only through colonial government that a reversion to this state of affairs can be prevented.

The effect consciously sought by colonialism was to drive into the natives' heads that if the settlers were to leave, they would at once fall back into barbarism, degradation and bestiality.[2]

In the long term, constant disparagement of the local culture creates self-doubt, saps the native's self-respect and so weakens resistance to foreign rule. The strategy of inferiorisation is fully successful when the native internalises the estimation of local culture which is propagated by the coloniser, acknowledging the superiority of metropolitan ways. The imperial refrain, which upholds the coloniser as the representative of civilisation, progress and universal human values, is then taken up by the *évolués*, those natives who try to escape from their backwardness by desperate identification with the culture of the metropolis.

To those who followed political debate in Scotland in the seventies, in the first crises of a developing nationalism (the SNP challenge and the devolution referendum struggle in 1979), parts of Fanon's account will have a familiar ring. For the cruder unionist ideologues did not shrink from using the kind of arguments identified by Fanon as strategies of colonialism. Scotland, it was often said, or implied, was an illiberal society, and the Scots a natively brutish and vicious people. Devolution, independence would be dangerous, since the Scots require the civilising hand of their southern neighbour (the English, within this mythology, being characterised by liberalism, tolerance, decency, etc).

'Scotching the Myths of Devolution', an article in *The Times* by Hugh Trevor-Roper, was one example of such argumentation. Writing at a time when Scottish independence seemed close, Trevor-Roper set out to describe the likely features of a separate Scottish state. His first guide is the condition of Scottish politics prior to 1707. 'The Scotch political system was a system of political banditry', whose sole principles were 'force and corruption'. The Scots were only liberated from these barbaric traditions by the Union and 'the removal of their national politics to London'. Thereafter they were able to enjoy the blessings of the British constitution, although the principles it embodies are essentially alien to Scottish culture: 'we ought to speak of the English constitution; for the Scots had no part in making it. The Scotch political system and political tradition. . . was quite different'.

To forestall the possible objection that the Scots might, in the meantime, have been turned into a less barbaric race, the author then presents what he takes to be contemporary evidence for his view that the Scots are by nature unfit to run a civilised polity:

.The pre-1707 tradition of Scotch government is not dead. . .
For 50 years of this century we have seen Scotch home rule
and are therefore able to see whether, or how far, its principles
have been changed in the interim. We have seen it at work
in the Scotch province of Ulster from 1922 till it had to be
suspended there too, in 1972. It is interesting to compare the
system of government in Scotland before 1707 and in Ulster
after 1922, and to see. . . certain resemblances, which I think
that I need not specify, but which bear eloquent testimony to
the well-known tenacity of the Scotch people.[3]

Other opponents of devolution sought to undercut the nationalist
case with the wonderfully simple argument that the Scots were not
even a nation. This move was also identified by Fanon: 'Every effort
is made to bring the colonised person . . . to recognise the unreality
of his "nation"'.[4] It will be recalled that such arguments were echoed
with particular fervour by our own *évolués*, members of parliament
and other minor luminaries of metropolitan institutions.

II

If the 'Scottish inferiority complex' has become a worthy of our
party small–talk, there has so far been no serious attempt to chart
the strategies and effects of inferiorisation in the Scottish context.
In what follows we want to identify certain instances of inferiorist
discourse. These are to be seen as particular manifestations of
an underlying code. This *langue* from which inferiorist texts are
generated can be characterised as a system of oppositions containing
the following terms:

Scotland	dark	England	enlightened
	backward		advanced
	fanatical		reasonable
	violent		decent
	barbaric		civilised
	illiberal		tolerant
	parochial		cosmopolitan
	uncouth		refined
	intemperate		moderate
	savage		mild
	unruly		orderly
	severe		kind
	harsh		gentle
	primitive		sophisticated

The mythology of inferiority has been most effective, perhaps, in our reading of the history of pre-Union Scotland. Fanon's model seems perfectly appropriate here. He speaks of 'the work of devaluing pre-colonial history'. Colonialist ideology:

> turns to the past of the oppressed people, and distorts, disfigures and destroys it . . . The total result looked for by colonial domination was indeed to convince the natives that colonialism came to lighten their darkness.[5]

Orthodox opinion about Scotland's condition prior to the Union — prior, that is, to the 'opening up' to English influence — has faithfully reflected Fanon's account of the imperial distortion of pre-colonial history. Darkness reigned. To quote Trevor-Roper once more:

> at the end of the seventeenth century, Scotland was a by-word for irredeemable poverty, social backwardness, political faction. The universities were the unreformed seminaries of a fanatical clergy.[6]

Scotland was, indeed, 'the rudest of all the European nations'.[7]

'Backward' and 'fanatical' are key terms in this discourse, which has informed the work of a host of Scottish historians throughout the years. H. G. Graham, in his *Social Life of Scotland in the Eighteenth Century* spoke of the 'austere, fanatic, religious character of Scotland', which was gradually eroded after 1707. James Young, a left-wing nationalist historian, refers in a recent book to the eighteenth-century Enlightenment dawning on 'a society with a centuries-old history of extreme backwardness'.[8]

The constant use of the metaphor of darkness and light, gloom and enlightenment to contrast pre- and post-Union Scotland underlines the crudity of such representations. Fantastic as they may be, however, these myths have acquired, thanks to endless repetition, the status of indubitable truth, and so are rarely subjected to critical analysis. They are passed on, from scholarly works, in textbooks and historical and political writing of a more popular kind to a wider audience. Here, for example, Andrew Cruickshank muses on the development of our national history:

> As the centuries pass by, they acquire a distinctive colour in the life of a nation. If we reckon these centuries since Copernicus, Galileo and Newton gave us a new view of the world, we could say that for Scotland the darkness of the seventeenth century gave way to the light and reason of the eighteenth.[9]

In his book *Devolution: the End of Britain?* Tam Dalyell MP
portrays the whole of Scottish history before 1707 as a kind of
nightmare from which union with England rescued the Scottish
people.

> Scotland was — as it had been throughout most of its history
> — violent, feud-ridden and torn apart by religious strife and
> dogmatism. The characteristic of this period was the Scots'
> lack of tolerance for one another.[10]
> . . .Scottish history before the union of the parliaments is a
> gloomy, violent tale of murders and tribal revenge . . . [11]

Fortunately, however, the Union and closer contact with the
civilised south transformed Scottish life. Centuries of barbarism
came to an abrupt end. Fanaticism and tribal warfare were replaced
by enlightenment and progress. Thus, after 1707, Dalyell informs
us:

> Edinburgh was no longer a claustrophobic provincial capital;
> opened to the influences of England she became one of the
> glories of European civilisation.[12]

The intellectual level of this contribution can be judged from the
fact that, two pages later, this picture of revolutionary change
is completely contradicted by the assurance that 'Scotland has
preserved her own identity and character' (violent, dogmatic, etc)
in spite of the Union. (*Plus ça change. . .*)

These views are rooted in a naive epistemology and philosophy
of history: the development of human belief as a progression from
superstition to reason, error to truth; history as progress, from
tribalism to civilisation, rudeness to politeness.

Incorporated in orthodox representations of Scotland's pre-union
history is an undifferentiated perception of Scottish Calvinism, as a
demonic, life-denying force. The destructive influence of Calvinism
on the development of Scottish culture and society is another key
motif of conventional historiography and cultural analysis. In the
third volume of H. T. Buckle's *History of Civilisation in England*,
published in 1861, the metropolitan view of the catastrophic effects
of Presbyterianism finds one of its classic expressions:

> In no civilised country is toleration so little understood as
> in Scotland. Nor can anyone wonder that such shall be the
> case who observes what is going on there. The churches
> are so crowded as they were in the middle ages and are
> filled with devout and ignorant worhshippers who flock
> together to listen to opinions of which the middle ages
> alone were worthy. The result is that there runs through
> the entire country a sour fanatical spirit, an aversion to

innocent gaiety, a disposition to limit the enjoyment of others. . .[13]

The judgment that Scotland was ruined by religion has become a truism of our cultural analysis. According to Fionn McColla, Calvinist antipathy to the arts 'snuffed out' our national culture. Since 'Knox and Melville clapped their preaching palms', Edwin Muir wrote in 'Scotland 1941', we have become a joyless, morbid nation, unresponsive to the aesthetic: 'a dull drove of faces harsh and vexed'. The idea that Calvinism represents a deep antipathy to art and culture, and that the Scots, as a result of this influence, are a philistine people, is now part of the stock-in-trade of our journalists and *littérateurs*. 'Where the arts are concerned', Anne Smith writes in the *New Statesman*, 'there is overwhelming evidence to suggest that the Scots prefer to go hungry at any time'; we are 'the culture-starved children of Knox'.[14] It seems necessary to insist, against this mindless endorsement of metropolitan prejudice, on the strengths of the Calvinist inheritance — moral seriousness, distrust of complacency, passion for theoretical argument (even if these are alien to the culture expressed by the London Sunday newspapers).

The Scots' sense of inferiority finds another outlet in the theory of Scottish inarticulacy, the Inarticulate Scot now being established alongside the Drunken Scot, the Repressed Scot and the Mean Scot in the mythology of the nation. The belief that Scots are tongue-tied in some distinctive way flourishes even among intellectuals inside the nationalist movement. P. H. Scott writes that our schools and universities, in suppressing Scots and Gaelic, 'made generations inarticulate and insecure'.[15] (It is strange that Scott accepts this idea so uncritically, since his article is concerned with the willingness of Scots to accept 'denigratory' views of Scottish culture, however implausible they might be. The author is here a victim of the credulity he is intent on criticising.) James Young believes that inarticulacy is a major malaise, like poverty and alcoholism a central, tragic feature of our national culture. In a typical analysis, he attributes inarticulacy to two main factors: an authoritarian social ethos coloured by repressive presbyterian attitudes, and 'the complete surrender to English culture' following the Union, when 'the enthusiasm of the Scottish elite in aping their superiors' entailed the imposition of English on the Scottish people. These pressures, in Young's view, have destroyed the possibility of natural and spontaneous expression in speech, creating a nation whose talk is halting and clumsy.[16]

Nationalists like Scott and Young find themselves in strange company on this issue. In an article entitled, significantly, 'The

Scottish Identity', Professor T C Smout depicts the Scots as a nation battered into speechlessness by an authoritarian educational system.

> The Scottish working class and middle class alike has [*sic*] been exposed for a century to a miserable Scottish education system (Scottish run, too) which believes that teaching consists of trying to smash facts into children. How can constructive consensus, adventure and innovation be produced in a society where phalanges of silent children arrive at the universities with their pens poised to catch truth as it drips from their teachers' lips?[17]

Here Scottish 'silence' is seen as part of a more general passivity and deference to authority, these qualities defining, it seems, in Smout's eyes, 'the Scottish identity'. A country whose schools can do no . better than this, he goes on, is hardly in a position to shape for itself a better future: 'Beating facts into children' is 'not a very effective way of promoting economic growth or anything else except anxiety and silence in the young'. (This essay was published in 1977, and the political context no doubt helps explain the intemperate tone. Still, it is remarkable that Smout should indulge publicly in such abuse.)

'The inarticulate Scot is socially created by an educational establishment which disapproves of the indigenous culture of the people', writes James Young. But he presents no persuasive support for his claim that Scots are inarticulate. Although he states that evidence exists, at most he cites other assertions that Scots are or were inarticulate. He also conflates inarticulacy with quite different phenomena, such as taciturnity and unwillingness to communicate. To use two of Young's own examples: neither an aversion to 'aimless talk', nor children's unwillingness, in the classroom, to 'speak and express their views' argues linguistic incapacity. Conversely, articulacy cannot be equated with verbosity.

Smout's argument that the Scots are a hopelessly cowed and passive people is likewise based on the flimsiest of premises. If it is true — and this would scarcely be surprising — that Scottish students at our anglicised universities are linguistically uncertain when confronted by a teacher and other students who speak RP (which is of course more prestigious than Scottish varieties of English), this hardly justifies the conclusion that Scots are tongue-tied or quiescent.

A comparison may be helpful here. In the USA there is a well-entrenched belief — propagated for many years by educational psychologists — that Negro speech is impoverished and that black children suffer, consequently, from 'verbal deprivation'. In a famous paper, W. Labov argued that what he calls 'the myth of verbal deprivation' is an expression of ignorance combined with class and racial prejudice; the theory 'has no basis in social reality'.[18] 'Scottish inarticulacy' has to be interpreted in the same way. It expresses the middle-class English prejudice that Scottish speech (and in particular Scottish working-class speech) is unrefined and defective (and voices the self-hatred of the *inferiorisés*, those who have been brought to believe in their own inferiority). The political force of the myth is clear; it is a component of an ideology which functions to undermine the self-belief of a dependent people.

Drawn to a cultural world in which Scottish traditions and practices carry little prestige, our intellectuals display a remarkable lack of sympathy for local culture. As far as Scottish popular culture is concerned, orthodox perceptions parallel the official accounts of Scotland's pre-union past, so that in the analysis of popular culture the images and tropes of inferiorist historiography return. The dominant view of local ways of life finds its archetypal expression in the phrase made popular by Christopher Harvie: 'black Scotland'.

From such perspectives, Scottish popular culture can be exhaustively described in terms of drink, football, tartanry and religion (understood as mindless religiosity). An inferiorist discourse here reinforces a particular kind of leftist politics, according to which the working class is essentially an oppressed group with little or no understanding of its situation, a repository of false consciousness.

Interest in Scottish popular culture has focused in the past few years on tartanry and its role in national consciousness. One of the key texts in this discussion is Tom Nairn's *Break-up of Britain*, where popular culture in Scotland is portrayed as deviant and deformed: 'an especially mindless popular culture revolving in timeless circles'. At the heart of this degenerate product is tartanry:

> Precisely because it has been unconnected with a 'higher' or normal, nationalist-style culture during the formative era of modern society, it (Scottish popular culture) has evolved blindly. The popular consciousness of separate identity, uncultivated by 'national' experience or culture in the usual sense, has become curiously fixed or fossilised on the level of the *image d'Épinal* and Auld Lang Syne, of the Scott Monument, Andy Stewart and the *Sunday Post* — to the point of forming a huge, virtually self-contained universe of *Kitsch*.[19]

This universe is embodied in

> that prodigious array of *Kitsch* symbols, slogans, ornaments, banners, war-cries, knick-knacks, music-hall heroes, icons, conventional sayings and sentiments. . . which have for so

long resolutely defended the name of 'Scotland' to the rest of the world. Annie S. Swan and Cronin provided no more than the relatively decent outer garb for this vast tartan monster. In their work the thing trots along doucely enough, on a lead. But it is something else to be with it (e.g.) in a London pub on International night, or in the crowd at the annual Military Tattoo in front of Edinburgh Castle. How intolerably vulgar! What unbearable, crass, mindless philistinism! One knows that *Kitsch* is a large constituent of mass popular culture in every land: but this is ridiculous![20]

The same sense of disgust informed the highly successful 'Scotch Myths' exhibition, mounted in 1981 by Barbara and Murray Grigor, an event designed to confront Scots with the awfulness of national popular culture. The exhibition underlined Nairn's view that tartan symbolism continues to dominate popular consciousness in Scotland, and that, in fulfilling a mystificatory function, it acts as an impediment to social and political change.

This position has also been reinforced in a number of recent articles. Writing in the *Bulletin of Scottish Politics*, Lindsay Paterson describes tartanry as the only set of signs Scots have at their disposal for the construction of a meaning of themselves and their country, 'the only mass, conscious symbols available to a people in search of its enduring sense of being a nation'. Tartanry thus 'continues to define Scottish culture in the eyes. . . of most Scots'. This is unfortunate, since these symbols offer no way of criticising existing society. They function, instead, to mystify; they prevent Scots from seeing themselves, their history and social reality with any clarity, and provide comfort and escape and false reasons for pride and satisfaction. Paterson describes tartanry as 'a bit of an opiate', 'an ideology to help people to adjust to their environment': ideal compensation for material deprivation.[21]

In an essay entitled 'Breaking the Signs: "Scotch Myths" as Cultural Struggle', Colin McArthur offers another variant of this argument. Tartanry is 'hegemonic at the level of popular consciousness'. It constitutes

a multi-faceted system of images and categories of thought into which Scots of the last century and a half have been — to use Althusser's term — interpellated, set in place as social actors, their consciousness being defined within the limits of this system.[22]

As in Paterson's contribution, tartanry is here presented as a form of false consciousness, false consciousness, so to speak, in its Scottish specificity. Given the power of this irrational discourse, socialist intellectuals in Scotland ought to be involved in deconstructing tartanry and in creating and ciculating alternative views of Scotland.

While these articles are skilful in analysing the world of tartanry, as accounts of what McArthur calls 'popular consciousness' they seem to us highly inadequate. They overlook, or ignore a major postulate of cultural analysis: that meanings are never passively consumed, but always subject to selection and adjustment to other discourses. There is in reality, no *Sunday Post* reader waiting to soak up the messages conveyed by D. C. Thomson, but only *Sunday Post readers*, people who are also trade unionists, or Kirk-goers, or nationalists, or defenders of animal rights, and their response to tartanry is not uncritical assimilation, but a complex negotiation dependent on the beliefs and values which are bound up with these other concerns.

The absence of any attempt to analyse the *reception* of tartan discourse, the failure to take into account the mediation of meaning, are serious flaws in these contributions. It is therefore possible for critics to question their estimation of the weight and role of tartanry in 'popular consciousness', and to argue, as P. H. Scott has done, that there are other myths about Scotland and the Scots which are more influential and more debilitating. 'The whole conception', Scott writes, referring to the Grigor exhibition, 'is based on too limited a view of the real nature of the myths which have undermined our self-confidence and bedevilled our political development'. The myth which really ought to be deconstructed, in Scott's view, is that 'Scotland before 1707 was backward, bloody and barbarous, that it was saved by the Union . . . and that thereafter economic progress and civilisation flowed benignly northwards from England'.[23] This critique can be taken a step further. The view that popular consciousness is dominated by tartanry, that the populace is sunk in ignorance and irrationality, accords perfectly with the governing image of Scotland as a dark and backward culture. This reflection allows us to locate the real significance of the discussion on tartanry, namely as another instance of the Scottish intellegentsia's readiness to embrace damning conceptions of national culture — in other words as an expression of inferiorism.

III

The darkness of pre-union Scotland, the catastrophic influence of Calvinism, Scottish inarticulacy, the peculiarly deformed character of Scottish popular culture — inferiorism is to be defined in terms of the potency of such obsessions. But there is another, equally significant phenomenon which must be taken into account here: the failure of the intellectuals to respond to Scottish traditions which cannot be assimilated to the paradigms of metropolitan culture.

The fate of Scottish traditions in philosophy is instructive in this respect. Philosophy departments in Scottish universities have become mere outposts of Anglo-American philosophy; and our intelligentsia seem entirely ignorant of Scottish philosophers who have resisted the specialising tendencies of this tradition, its break with philosophy in the Continental style, and its retreat to concern with issues remote from social and political life. A central task of cultural nationalism is the recovery of Scottish cultural practices (like these native philosophical traditions) which have been submerged by the intelligentsia's adoption of English cultural modes.

In this essay we have tried to indicate the main outlines of our subject: the disposition of the Scottish intelligentsia to accept metropolitan assessments of Scottish life, which inevitably misjudge its character and potential and automatically codify specifically Scottish culture as inferior to metropolitan styles. Inferiorism is then expressed, in more precise terms, in the adoption of discourses which portray Scotland as a dark and backward corner of the land, and in the severe distrust of Scottish traditions and precedents displayed by the intellectuals. Combatting this dismal orientation will mean, then, on the one hand, interrogating official discourses on Scotland, and, on the other, re-asserting the practices which define our own culture.

2

Scotland in History: Inferiorist Historiography

No one should believe that over-attention to the past of a nation — even a nation in danger of cultural eclipse — will breathe life into its present or its future. But if a national culture is to remain alive, its history too must live in some distinctive way and must be perceived as integral to the lives of those who share in it. This helps to define their sense of collective identity, gives them their confidence, lets them know where they are.

This is what, socially and politically speaking, invests the past with its value.

Yet there are grounds for arguing that large tracts of the Scottish past have been affected in ways reminiscent of the distortive action of colonialism upon 'third world' cultures.

In the colonial experience, the native past came to be portrayed as one of barbarism, a past with which no sane and civilised person could conceivably wish to claim relation. As we have seen, Frantz Fanon has discovered and traced the crudely distortive operation of this historiography on the past of the African cultures:

> Colonialism, which has not bothered to put too fine a point on its efforts, has never ceased to maintain that the Negro is a savage. . . For colonialism this vast continent was the haunt of savages, a country riddled with superstitions and fanaticism, destined for contempt. . . The contention by colonialism [was] that the darkest night of humanity lay over pre-colonial history. . .[1]

The adoption and adaptation of these views by the native educated groups produces a particularly contorted attitude of mind, an inferiorist perspective upon the history of their own culture.

Though not always in so crude a form, projections of this kind are to be traced in much of the scholarship associated with different aspects of Scottish history. They do not suddenly appear in a fully refined form at a particular historical juncture, expressed by a particular writer or group of thinkers. The matter is much more subtle, and much more insidious.

I

Some of the attitudes to pre-Union Scottish society expressed by 'assimilationist' Scottish intellectuals in the age of the Enlightenment bear similarities to more recent attitudes we would wish to describe as inferiorised. And the conception of traditional Scottish culture published to the world through the vast influence of Walter Scott, while sympathetic in many ways, lent itself to misinterpretation by contemporary intellectuals concerned to dismiss as culturally worthless whatever was without value to the Industrial Age.

Yet the views reflected in the works of both these periods were at least equivocal and could not be said to have brought about a significant loss of confidence in Scottish society and culture as things stood by the time of the Disruption.

However, it has recently been suggested that many of our historical conventions, and historiographic 'spectacles' may have been manufactured as recently as late-Victorian times. Certainly in influential works of this period, a new, well-defined and quite unequivocal perception of the history of Scottish society emerges. This can quite confidently be identified in H. G. Graham's widely-respected *Social Life of Scotland in the Eighteenth Century*, first published in 1889. It should be a matter of some astonishment how influential this work still is in some historical circles. In any event, historiographically, it is a seminal work.

Although he is purportedly writing of the eighteenth century, much of the book is actually a commentary on the pre-Union Scottish world. And for Graham, this involved him in a commentary upon a Dark Age.

It is clear from the 'Preface' onward, that Graham regarded the Union as the principal agent of civilising this ancient, idiosyncratic, and unquestionably *passé* culture. Besides the two (backward-looking) Rebellions, he conceived the Union as the only "outstanding event" in eighteenth-century Scottish history. In the century which followed it:

> there was a continuous revolution going on — a gradual transformation in manners, customs, opinions, among every class; the rise and progress of agricultural, commercial, and intellectual energy, that turned waste and barren tracts to fertile fields — stagnant towns to centres of busy trade — a

lethargic, slovenly populace to an enterprising race — an utterly impoverished country to a prosperous land. These facts constitute *the real history* of the Scots in the eighteenth century.[2]

The notion of an all-embracing change turning upon, or at least instigated by the Union is a central theme in this historiographic explanation.

It is certain that P. Hume Brown's collection *Early Travellers in Scotland*[3] was instrumental in confirming this view of things, containing as it did highly critical accounts either of seventeenth/early eighteenth century Lowland Scotland written by visiting Englishmen, or of the Highlands in the eighteenth century by Englishmen or Lowland Scots with an 'Improving' ideology to sustain. Hume Brown himself recognised the imbalance of the source book he had created but it has been used without the caution or qualification its compiler would have advised.

The historiographic view which begins to emerge from Graham is considered to have much to commend it by British metropolitan historians who take an interest in the history of the Scottish natives. H.R. Trevor-Roper has been known to express the view that Graham's book is the last decent history of Scotland written by a Scotsman. In his own work he has conceived of the major characteristic of seventeenth century Scottish culture as a demonic Calvinism, presenting the period as almost exclusively associated with intolerance and persecution, devoid of cultural value save in the Episcopalian North-East.[4] Yet this is a view very widely held by Scottish intellectuals too — and one which at least partly derives from historical judgements purveyed by another late nineteenth century historian, H.T. Buckle.

Buckle portrayed seventeenth century Scotland as a culture overshadowed by 'the worst kind of superstition', a special, almost unique 'Scotch superstition', never previously seen in history (save in the worst excesses of the Spanish Inquisition) and surely never to be seen again. The initial balance of historical judgement early in Buckle's main chapter on the seventeenth century is quickly overwhelmed by a furious tirade against the Scots clergy and Scottish Calvinism, 'one of the most detestable tyrannies ever seen on earth':

> Under the influence of this horrible creed, and from the unbounded sway exercised by the clergy who advocated it, the Scotch mind was thrown into such a state, that, during the seventeenth, and part of the eighteenth century some of the noblest feelings of which our nature is capable, the feelings

of hope, of love, and of gratitude, were set aside, and were replaced by the dictates of a servile and ignominious fear.[5]

For Buckle (who is clearly deeply emotionally entangled in his own historical researches and argument) these judgements are projected on to the Scots character in general, which is associated with the distorted, queer, unnatural: 'thus it was, that the national character of the Scotch was, in the seventeenth century, dwarfed and mutilated.'[6]

This ultimately underpins a general historical perspective on the seventeenth century, and one almost inevitably couched in those tropes and metaphors involving the contrast of darkness and light so frequently to be found in the historiography of seventeenth and eighteenth century Scotland:

> A state of society so narrow and so one-sided, has never been seen in any other country equally civilized. Nor did there appear much chance of abating this strange monopoly. As the seventeenth century advanced, the same train of events was continued; the clergy and the people always making common cause against the crown, and being, by the necessity of self-preservation, forced into the most intimate union with each other. . . for upwards of a century [the preachers'] exertions stopped all intellectual culture, discouraged all independent enquiry, made men in religious matters fearful and austere, and coloured the whole national character with that dark hue, which, though now gradually softening, it still retains.[7]

Buckle, of course, was concerned to establish a hypothesis which emphasised *one* line of continuity between the deductivist bias which, in his view, had dominated theology in the earlier period but then disastrously survived in the secular metaphysics and general culture of the Scottish 'Enlightenment'. Yet by the end of his work, his use of historical material has been such as to establish in Scottish cultural history the same Manichean contrasts centering on the turn of the eighteenth century, as we have found in Graham's account of Scottish social history, over the same period:

> I have now completed my examination of the Scotch intellect as it unfolded itself in the seventeenth and eighteenth centuries. The difference between those two periods must strike every reader. In the seventeenth century the ablest Scotchmen wasted their energies on theological subjects. . .It was natural that a literature should be created. . . which encouraged superstition, intolerance, and bigotry; a literature full of dark misgivings, and of still darker threats . . . a

literature in a word, which, spreading gloom on every side, soured the temper, corrupted the affections, numbed the intellect, and brought into complete discredit those bold and original inquiries, without which there can be no advance in human knowledge, and consequently no increase of human happiness. To this, the literature of the eighteenth century offered a striking and most exhilarating contrast. It seems as if, *in a moment, all was changed*. The Baillies, the Billings. . . and the rest of that monkish rabble, were succeeded by eminent and enterprising thinkers, whose genius lighted up every department of knowledge, and whose minds, fresh and vigorous as the morning, opened for themselves a new career, and secured for their country a high place in the annals of European intellect.[8]

In the first half of this century, leading historical works have continued to reflect these assumptions. From the first sentence of Henry Hamilton's influential *Industrial Revolution in Scotland* we are presented with the picture of an abrupt, multi-faceted transformation in Scottish affairs, turning on the year 1707 and the decades which followed:

> In this book I have tried to show how Scottish economic life was revolutionized in the course of the eighteenth and nineteenth centuries . . . and especially to show how Scotland *was transformed from a country with a primitive agriculture* interwoven with industry . . . to one distinguished for its progressive farming and extensive textile industries . . . My story begins in the early eighteenth century, when the Union had opened up to Scotland vast opportunities. . .
> [9]

The vocabulary of total transformation in commerce and agriculture, and in particular the agency of the union in bringing this about, is repeatedly emphasised in the Preface and Introduction, thus defining the reader's general context:

> The passing of the Scots Parliament to Westminster in 1707 heralded a new era in the history of Scotland. It was an event of the most tremendous importance . . . [Scotland] was presented with boundless opportunities, and infinitely poor as she was she rose to the occasion. This in itself involved a revolution in the commerce of the country.
> [10]

The concepts of the industrial and agricultural 'revolutions' which (though less fashionable than formerly) are associated in the history of England with general socio-economic changes stretching over lengthy periods, are related here to a single event in Scottish history, to the watershed of 1707.

II

At first glance more recent economic historians have not relied on this pattern to structure their presentation of Scotland's story. Indeed Anand Chitnis has suggested that 'social and economic historians have been in the forefront of those who have countered the impression that seventeenth-century Scottish history is an entirely dark age'. He is referring, mainly, to R. H. Campbell and T. C. Smout. His praise in both cases is over-fulsome.

It is true that Campbell has stood out from this whole historiographic canon, and attempted an alternative interpretation, at least in relation to cultural history and the Scottish Enlightenment. He has presented a direct challenge to the general view, not only in offering a sympathetic portrayal of 17th century Scottish Calvinism, but in acknowledging an interpretation which conceives of its central significance in the formation of the characteristic 'psychological' and 'sociological' nature of the work of the Scottish *philosophes*. Chitnis (whose own work, it should be acknowledged, reflects these ideas) has summarised the position:

> Theology in Scotland was the original social science, and had been stressed and elaborated throughout the seventeenth century to encourage the transformation of the individual who, through his conduct in life towards others, was endeavouring to attain salvation. That conduct towards others expressed itself in the multifarious relationships and categories of relationship (political, legal, economic) that existed in society and ideally was a precondition for social change. Theology was therefore a social science, which in the seventeenth century paved the way for the secular social sciences of the eighteenth century. The contribution of churchmen to the Scottish Enlightenment, which was so productive of works on social philosophy, was well founded and in a sound tradition. Earlier, for example, George Buchanan (1506–82) had graced Scottish Church history . . . and had been renowned for such scholarly works of political theory as *De jure Regni apud Scotos* (1579) and a history of Scotland.[11]

However, Campbell articulated these views largely in two short essays produced in the mid-1970s, and published to the world through vehicles unlikely to project them to much prominence. He

has been much more influential as a more specifically socio-economic
historian through his well-known (and perhaps significantly titled)
Scotland Since 1707. In his Preface, Campbell describes this work as
'a general introduction to the chief forces which have determined the
growth of the industrial society that is modern Scotland'. However,
though apparently keen to shake off the historiographic outlook
we have been considering, he succeeds merely in obfuscating
the significance of the year 1707 itself and actually reinforces
the traditional conception of the Union as the *primum mobile* of
'modern Scotland'.

He emphasises that both before and after the Union it was clear
that 'Scotland's economic backwardness' could only be overcome by
imitation of English example:

> The Union did effect a difference sufficient to classify it as
> an epoch-making event in Scottish economic history . . .
> [it] effected an internal change in the means of remedying
> Scotland's economic backwardness by ensuring that Scottish
> economic policy aimed at rivalling the achievements of
> the English economy through complementary rather than
> competitive action.[12]

The notion of historical continuity interrupted by a fundamental
transformation is constantly reiterated: 'Emulation of English ways
and achievements inevitably implied a social transformation before
modern industrial techniques could be applied . . .' For Campbell,
despite a brief acknowledgement of some 17th century agricultural
development, a profound change, a 'transformation' in the entire
'structure of the Scottish economy' turned on the year 1707 and the
Union.

It might reasonably have been expected that Scottish intellectuals
of a more leftward and nationalist bent would have been concerned
to re-examine these hoary historiographic notions, and perhaps
fashion new patterns to aid our understanding of Scottish history.
Yet in the work of Tom Nairn, the most impressive and serious
left theorist of the sixties and seventies we find distilled from the
great vat of his confessedly secondary-source knowledge, in a near
pure form, the primary elements of this world-view. Following the
Union, Scottish society 'took off towards a revolutionary condition
of industrialization'.

> As a part of this advance, there occurred a significant
> florescence of Scottish national culture. *In comparison with
> the theocratic gloom of the 17th century*, this appeared strange
> even to some of its protagonists. . . Concentrated in such
> a small area and time, in a land *transported so incredibly*

quickly out of Barbarity into Civility (the philosophes) were the chief exemplars of the European Enlightenment's view of Progress.

At this point one can see how important the temporal dimension is for any model of Scottish society. For, in *the extraordinary favourable conditions of the Union the rapid progress* of Scotland's new, bourgeois civil society cannot help appearing 'premature' . . . Few, even among perfervid nationalists, would regret that the country escaped so smartly from the age of witch-burning and feudal futility. But in relation to virtually every other region in Europe, *Scottish advance was precocious.* In a number of decisive respects, the Scots had crossed the great divide of basic 'development' before the real nature of the problem had even presented itself.[13]

Nairn's use of eighteenth century orthographic convention should not be construed as indicating that this account is merely an extended cultural criticism playing ironically upon the language and assumptions of Enlightenment 'conjectural history'. On the contrary it fundamentally reflects his own understanding of the history of early modern Scotland: indeed the suddenness and precocity of this transformation in the conditions obtaining throughout Scottish society are absolutely central to his marxist variant on this traditional historiography.

Only a very small number of Scottish historians, writing mostly (and significantly) during the past fifteen years, have valiantly attempted to offer an alternative perspective. A larger group, particularly those in the sub-specialty Departments of Scottish History, have simply ignored the exercise of this cultural power, either by limiting themselves to the reservations of medieval and Reformation history or by adopting a strictly empirical approach. Well-known and prolific figures like Gordon Donaldson and William Ferguson are amongst those who appear to have adopted such strategies.

For the rest, the Scottish intelligentsia has uncritically purveyed a perspective on their national history which is very economically conveyed in the first sentence of A.J. Youngson's much-praised *Making of Classical Edinburgh.* Reflecting on Edinburgh's architectural splendours Youngson observes that they owed much 'to the late and sudden flowering of Scottish culture, when as Balfour put it, a country which had done nothing up to the eighteenth century, after the eighteenth century began seemed almost to do everything'.[14]

III

The pre-eminence of this view of Scottish history is reflected and confirmed in the appearance of similar perspectives in recent American works which (like Nairn's) have relied on secondary sources. Setting the scene for his study of *James McCosh and the Scottish Intellectual Tradition* (1981), J. D. Hoeveler observes that in the eighteenth century:

> As never before the country was prosperous. . . Greatly responsible for *the transformation* was the famous 1707 Act of Union that joined Scotland and England into Great Britain . . . Evidence of Scotland's *emergence from the economic dark ages* appeared everywhere, perhaps most strikingly in the rural areas where agricultural improvements made Scotland the envy of Europe.[15]

This notion of a near-apocalyptic change in socio-economic affairs is equally projected as the proper framework for understanding what happened in the religious and cultural spheres. It was, we learn, with the early eighteenth century, and Francis Hutcheson's occupation of the Glasgow chair of philosophy that 'Scotland began to emerge from the glacial age of Calvinism'. A sudden and astonishing thaw it was to be: for just before the union:

> as religious extremism flourished in the 1690s there was little indication how near at hand was the great transformation of Scottish life and culture. In fact, though, Scotland was at the dawning of a new age.[16]

(One can hardly blame the American for his adoption of the weary metaphor of the night and the dawn used so characteristically by those sharing this historiographic 'vision').

The same conception of a sudden and total change, this time more directly related to cultural history, is projected in Charles Camic's study of the major figures of the Scottish Enlightenment, *Experience and Enlightenment* (1983).[17] As is typical of this entire historiographic explanation, Camic establishes a sharp contrast between the pre-and post-Union Scottish world. The culture of seventeenth and early eighteenth century Scotland was 'both deeply Calvinist and at the same time, thoroughly pervaded by medieval attitudes of particularism and dependency'. A society in this 'backward condition' could not contribute to the remarkable cultural achievements of eighteenth century Scotland. The productions of the 'enlighteners' must be separated from the backwardness and darkness which obtained before the early eighteenth century. Their achievement is in fact seen as 'a revolutionary rift with the culture that had held sway in Scotland since the Reformation'. Camic insists (echoing many interpretations of the Scottish Enlightenment) that these Scottish intellectuals, raised almost entirely within Scottish Calvinist culture and happy to spend most of their lives within it, produced a series of remarkable ideas and works which had no relation whatever to the past history or contemporary modes of that culture. (It is not surprising to find that a major source of Camic's knowledge of seventeenth century Scotland, and Scottish Calvinism, is H. G. Graham).

IV

The development of alternative views of the Scottish past is rendered difficult in face of the social and cultural power within the intelligentsia of English intellectuals who update and embellish the traditional inferiorising view in contemporary works. The acclaim accorded these studies by British metropolitan academics and reviewers gives them disproportionate influence within Scottish history circles — especially in our anglicised Universities where the views of the London and Oxbridge reviewers are *sans pareil*.

The leading figure among these outposted metropolitans is probably T. C. Smout whose best-known work *A History of the Scottish People*, carries astonishing weight as an account of the Scottish past.

Smout is too sophisticated an historian to reflect this historiography in a crude fashion. Indeed he apparently dissociates himself from those historians whose work suggests a crude discontinuity in Scottish history, centering on the Union (though the continuity Smout emphasises is a continuity of assimilation, of increasing identity with 'Britain', not one of difference).

Nevertheless, a closer inspection reveals a recurring rhythm or pattern in the structure of Smout's main chapters on the seventeenth century.

His chapters on rural life are considered more fully in the context of the next chapter. However they do reflect the pattern of his chapters on the seventeenth century. His account of the life-experience of the different social strata, and of rural trade, is well-presented and interesting though drawn from sources, and made the subject of contemporary comparisons which it would anticipate the next chapter to criticise here. But as he reaches

the end of his account, the most depressing aspects of seventeenth
century social history — the periodic slumps culminating in the
famines in the 1690's — are emphasised, less to underscore the
historical account or even make a general historiographical point
than, in a schoolmasterly final paragraph, to adjure those concerned
with Scottish history to remember the character of the Scottish past
before the eighteenth century:

> It is fitting to end our chapter on rural life with the memories
> of these things. It was the cyclical recurrence of apparently
> inevitable catastrophe which determined so much of the
> fatalism and hopelessness of peasant existence in the centuries
> before 1690. It was the deliverance from these conditions that
> was the most important work of the economic revolution in the
> centuries afterwards. Those who are tempted to romanticise
> the Scottish past would do well to meditate on the 1690s.[18]

The main body of Smout's succeeding chapter on urban life
again provides, on the basis of his sources, an interesting account
of the different social groups in the towns and of the character
of burgh organisation. However, in his final pages he concludes
with an account of the reduction to serfdom of a (proportionately
fairly small) number of colliers and salters in the east Lowlands.
This occurrence is compared unfavourably to the situation in
England where, although the industries were similarly organised,
the sturdy commons maintained their liberty. Once again, this way
of structuring the chapter permits Smout to deprecate seventeenth
century Scottish society and to hold up an admonitory finger to any
who might consider an alternative perspective:

> Seventeenth century society did not protest either in 1606,
> in 1641, in 1660 or in 1690. . .The lot of the inarticulate
> industrial serfs should give the political historians of Scotland
> pause for reflection. In what senses can the civil wars, the
> covenants, and the revolutions of the seventeenth century
> be held to be about the basic liberties of man when all
> the contenders paused in the struggle to confirm, as a
> matter of automatic common-sense, the serfdom of the least
> privileged?[19]

(It should be said that nothing in Smout's account could be held to
justify the final assertion in this paragraph.)

The first part of Smout's final chapter on this period considers
certain of the major literary and scientific figures and also assesses
Scottish cultural achievements in the traditions of ballad and court
poetry, architecture and silver-working. It is an appreciative general
account, and a first-class introduction for anyone who might wish

to pursue their interest further. Again, however, the final part of
the chapter consists of a lengthy account of the witch-craze and
persecution of the period. There is no doubt that an account of
these strange and terrible social outbursts should be included in any
general history of the period. But the sustained account at this point
in the book seems to obliterate the cultural achievements described
earlier in the chapter, and leaves the reader with the impression of
a century dominated by intolerance, torture and superstition merely
overlaid by a thin veneer of literary, scientific and architectural
achievements.

Despite his efforts at providing a more balanced account, Smout's
version of seventeenth-century developments leaves the reader not
with a rounded conception of an early-modern society attempting
economic change in various directions, coping with major threats
to social cohesion and achieving particular cultural expression, but
with the impression of a society if not founded upon, at least
characterised by economic catastrophe, serfdom and superstition.

This presentation of seventeenth century Scotland allows Smout
to advance a familiar explanation (even couched in familiar
metaphor) of what brought about 'The Age of Transformation':

> The eighteenth century began in an atmosphere of gloom and
> despondency, in a trade depression, the shadow of famine
> and the crushing news of the loss of the [Darien] colony
> . . . Within five years of the final dénouement at Darien,
> however, events had taken a new turn with the achievement
> of the Union of Parliaments'.[20]

Although Smout acknowledges that it would take several decades
for the benefits to be fully realised, he is quite clear as to the
causes of the growing enlightenment throughout Scottish social and
cultural life:

> With the wisdom of historical hindsight we can see that
> Scotland was beginning to move with England towards the
> watershed of the industrial revolution: we can see that the
> movement depended partly on the Union, and . . . [partly
> on] stimuli that originated in England . . . In the place of
> passive resignation to poverty, there was a lightening of the
> spirit that showed *through every aspect of Scottish life and
> culture*[21]

It is remarkable how instantly pervasive were the effects on
Scotland of the events which took place in 1707 in the Parliament
House, involving (in proportion to the Scottish population) a small
number of landowners and gentry. It would seem that, in this
historiography, Namierism is far from dead.

Other assimilationist and anglicised historians — often congenital
metropolitans condemned to life on the cultural periphery — echo
the assumption that the character and intensity of change which
they perceive as occurring at the turn of the eighteenth century
is inexplicable in terms of 'normal' historical process, so much so
that at times they can only describe it in supra-natural terms. It is
as though they cannot believe the possibility of their own assertions:

> The history of eighteenth-century Scotland offers its historians
> the most noble prospects. In that century Scotland was bound
> to England by the sort of incorporating union that has been so
> often projected in European history, and which has so often
> failed. By the middle of the century she had at last found
> the political stability which had for long eluded her and was
> entering a period of economic growth *little short of miraculous*
> for its speed and intensity.[22]

Here N. T. Phillipson and R. Mitchison set the scene as editors
of the influential collection of essays, *Scotland in the Age of
Improvement*. The alchemy is of course considered to extend to
the sphere of cultural history and

> the time of the Scottish enlightenment, *that remarkable outburst*
> of intellectual life in which, *almost overnight*, Scotland was
> snatched from the relative cultural isolation in which she had
> passed the seventeenth century and placed in the centre of the
> thinking world. [23]

For those with this kind of perspective, historical significance or
meaning is very much a matter of being 'placed in the centre of the
thinking world'; and it is possible to understand how, according to
this reasoning, the — even fleeting — cultural centrality of Scottish
thought could only be explained by a cataclysmic change, an
abnormal leap forward in the development of a backward periphery
permitting its (temporary) irruption into History.

Characteristically, the credibility of this explanation is supported
by an undifferentiated denigration of the seventeenth century.
Scottish historians are admonished not to pay too much attention
to Jacobitism and :

> to the movements within the Kirk which attempted to keep
> in the forefront of men's minds the narrow sectarian and
> theocratic issues of the seventeenth century. [24]

Pre-union Scotland is sweepingly described as in 'a state of near
anarchy', and described, astonishingly, as 'an unruly country'.

The cultural arrogance of all of this would be remarkable enough
without the knowledge that these views emerge in a continuous flow
from a strata of English or anglicised academics *within the country*,

indeed within the very universities of the culture whose history they so disdain; and were it not for the fact that their views have been so slavishly adopted and developed by an inferiorised native intelligentsia.

V

Though not always explicit, this general historiographic perspective continues to underpin fundamental Unionist assumptions about Scotland and the mass of her people. It certainly contributed to some of the most influential and powerfully-placed opposition to the recent independence movement:

> If the Nationalists wish to be emotional and romantic, and avoid the history of the more immediate past by harking back to the Forty-five, or pre-Union times. . . then surely those of us who take a different view may be pardoned if we are equally selective in our choice of historical instances, and why should we not with reasonable justification concentrate on, say, the last two hundred years and call attention to some of the benefits of the Union.[25]

This was the perspective of the secretary to the University of Edinburgh in the late sixties and early seventies. Certainly in the works of the academics themselves, and in those of the wider Scottish intelligentsia, the chief characteristics of this historiography re-emerge.

The seventeenth century (when Scotland is projected as still largely autonomous) is subject to an undifferentiated devalorisation and vilification. It is described in terms of primitiveness, superstition and, generally, cultural and economic backwardness. It was a time 'before the Dawn', before even 'The Prelude to the Take-off', before 'the escape', before the 'emergence from the glacial age', before 'the real history of the Scots'. It was a time of the psychologically contorted, the culturally deformed, the politically factious — an 'unruly' time before ordered History, before Civilisation.

The emergence, escape, dawn, take-off etc, are conceived as of startling precocity, near-incredible even to the historians themselves, and involve a total transformation centering on, or initiated by the incorporating Union of 1707 with England. This leads directly to economic *development*, socio-political *order* and cultural *enlightenment*. There occurs an alchemic transmutation of a base-metal culture into glittering gold.

The power of this undifferentiated and Manichean conception of Scottish history, and its distortive effect on the way the Scots perceive their own past requires to be traced in each sphere of history. This is a massive task. It would necessitate a scale of resources and an institutional base not surprisingly unavailable to those who would challenge the colonisation of Scottish culture and the descent of its academics and intellectuals into inferiorism. However the next chapter seeks to at least point the way, taking as its subject the sphere of rural history. This is not inappropriate in considering a nation which, whatever else it was before the early 19th century, was predominantly a rural society.

3

The Darkness and the Dawn:
Perceptions of Scottish Rural History

We have referred to the significance of H. G. Graham's *Social Life of Scotland* in the formation of the historiography described in the last chapter. In focussing now on rural history, the most cursory examination of Graham's early chapters (devoted largely to rural life) reveals assumptions and judgements which have deeply coloured subsequent historical work. Graham begins his account with the 'waste and barren tracts' — with the land, the topography itself. Comment has already been made on the influence of travellers' accounts (often drawn from Hume Brown's *Early Travellers in Scotland*) in defining the perspectives which would be adopted by later historians. From the beginning, Graham's projection of this landscape is as seen through the eyes of 'the few Englishmen who journeyed to North Britain, . . . with the air of heroic courage with which a modern traveller sets forth to explore the wild region of *a savage land*'. There follows a sustained description of the 'bleak and bare' countryside: even the better houses looked only upon 'some bare and ugly moor', the practice of planting trees around country houses only becoming common 'after the Union, when the eyes of Scots gentlemen were opened to English ways'.[1]

This projection of the landscape is repeatedly reinforced:

> The country presented in those days little that was picturesque to the eye of the English traveller as he rode precariously by the roads that were but ill-made tracks on which his horse could barely keep its footing . . . It was treeless and bare; the land was marshy and full of bogs; instead of meadows with flocks feeding were wild moors stretching far and wide.[2]

Consonant with the aesthetically displeasing landscape is 'the *barbarous* mode of its agriculture'. This phrase prefigures a standard terminology in considering pre-improvement agricultural technology.

Describing the pre-Union forms, Graham's language is all of the backward, the primitive, the unrefined, constructing a series of connected images of pre-civilisation. In the process of producing food from grain, 'every operation was primitive, involving a maximum of labour with a minimum of profit'. The traditional technique used in the seventeenth century production of pot barley was a 'savage process', a 'primitive method'; while the seventeenth century process of separating oat grains from the husks, was 'a still more barbarous method'. We are presented with a picture of a rural society which has not emerged from prehistoric times: 'The methods of tillage were supremely clumsy and primitive. The ploughs were enormous, unwieldy constructions . . .'.

Such severe judgements on the barrenness of the topography and backwardness of the farming are gradually extended to more obviously anthropogenic aspects of the landscape including the architecture of the rural buildings. The source of these judgements remains obvious:

> With the bleak and barren landscape and the meagre and shabby living of the people their dwellings were in painful harmony. In 1702 Morer, the English chaplain, described the houses of the vulgar as 'low and feeble', 'their walls made of a few stones jumbled together.'[3]

Graham alludes repeatedly through the book to the people's 'hovels'. He is rather more appreciative of the occasional great castellated houses, but has little time for the ordinary country mansion 'devoid of dignity from the floor to the corbel-stepped gable roof'. In the disappearance of the majority of seventeenth-century country mansions, 'the country lost little in picturesqueness, for very many had been hopelessly commonplace, with little that was quaint . . .' and with little of the civilised artifice of park or garden.

The reproduction of the English travellers' accounts of the landscape as ugly and threatening, of the land as agriculturally 'underdeveloped' and of the rural architecture as aesthetically displeasing, anticipates an equally contemptuous portrayal of the people themselves.

The historian sympathises with the disgust of the English traveller in passing through regions 'where the inhabitants spoke an uncouth dialect, were dressed in rags, lived in hovels, and fed on grain with which [the Englishman] fed his horses'. Graham's historical account of the native peasantry invariably adopts the perspective and values of the visiting observers who are his sources — the perspective of civilised and rational men casting their eyes upon the aboriginal and the deformed:

> Equal marks of poverty met the traveller's eye in the natives clad in blue rags, their skin browned with dirt, their gait

listless; in the horses — dwarfish, lean and hungry; the cattle, emaciated and stunted; the miserable hovels of turf and stone; the poor patches of tilled land, abounding in thistles and nettles in the ridges.[4]

(Indeed the vocabulary of deformation — of the deviant or the distorted — often figures in Graham's descriptions of social forms which remained 'ineffaceably Scottish'. The survivals of pre-assimilation Scottish society were characterised by a 'peculiarity' of character, an 'oddity of life'. Graham considered Kay's portraits of the lawyers captured this particularly well:

a veritable menagerie of oddities, chokeful of whims, absurdities, and strange idiosyncrasies, and of queer humour, conscious or unconscious, in dignitaries without dignity.[5])

This deformity remained, too, in country houses and manses 'in spite of the advent of modern innovations, and that frequent intercourse with the wider world which was fast polishing the race into conventional shape'. It is interesting to note that Graham's conception of the backwardness of the native rural dwellers does not differentiate by social class: 'every improvement was slow and obstinately resisted by an impecunious gentry and a lethargic and timid tenantry'.

However, it is the mass of the rural population for whom the most denigratory and vitriolic descriptions are reserved. Once again these are largely based on the accounts and judgements of the English travellers:

The sluggishness of the labourers had passed into proverbs and by-words. Kay, the naturalist, in 1660, was struck by the habit of the ploughmen putting on their cloaks when they set a-ploughing. . . and the same slothfulness struck Pennant, the traveller, more than a century later. The Scottish clergy deplored and English visitors ridiculed the poverty-stricken aspect of the peasantry: their pinched faces, wrinkled features, tattered dress, and foul skin and fouler habits.[6]

'Ignorance and stupidity' are projected as the characteristics of the Scots rural population together with an attraction to the filthiest conditions and coarsest of clothing. Even piety failed to disturb 'the inveterate sluggishness of farmer and labourer: it seemed rather to dignify dirt and to consecrate laziness'. On the contrary, 'religious feelings and Christian ordinances ministered to idleness, fostered prejudice, and depressed and hampered agriculture'.

Neither will Graham permit any other explanations to modify the severity of his judgements upon the psychological-racial traits of the pre-assimilation Scots population. He rejects the proposition (despite citing a good deal of evidence for it) that the prevalence of short leases may have discouraged change:

> the hesitation to alter old methods was less due to want of security of reaping the fruit of their labour, than to *prejudice, indolence, and obstinacy* in retaining old and easy customs.[7]

Among the Highlanders who 'swarmed' in the northern glens this absence of drive, this racial failure of will was even more pronounced:

> even those who were fishers were too lazy to pursue their occupation, except when driven to it by necessity. . . . They loitered through their summers and idled out the winters in congenial inactivity scorching their feet at the peat fires. . . as they lay on the floor. [8]

Nothing characterised the backwardnesss of either Lowland or Highland rural Scots so much as their immersion in 'Superstition'. This is dealt with at some length and refers to the people's liking for folk tales and legends and their enactment of old stories and songs on social occasions. In Graham's account it is complemented by their adherence to a 'grim creed' dominated by 'austerity and fanaticism'. The historian's perception of the inter-mixture of formal religion and folk legend in early-modern communities is surely accurate, but his terminology and tone are such that his observations serve to reinforce the pre-civilised character which he projects upon pre-assimilation Scottish society.

II

In the first half of the twentieth century Scottish economic history was not conspicuously well served, and certainly agrarian history, in particular, received scant attention. However, the standard texts which were available such as Henry Hamilton's *Industrial Revolution in Scotland* continued to reflect the historiographic perspective encountered in Graham. This is absolutely explicit in relation to agricultural revolution and improvement:

> The throwing open of this enormously important market in 1707 naturally soon had the effect of directing attention to the improvement of agriculture. . . The improving movement. . . commenced in some parts of the country shortly after the Union. . . [9]

As in Graham, the landscape is projected as little more than a 'mere waste', a 'desert', by drawing on the descriptions of the improvers. And the pre-civilised character of pre-Union agricultural methods is emphasised: 'at the opening of the eighteenth century the methods of agriculture in Scotland were very primitive. . . The implements of tillage were ludicrous'. The harrows, he observes, quoting Lord Kames, were 'more fit to raise laughter than to raise soil' — while he considered that the harness was 'of the most primitive kind, ropes backbands and traces being twisted from (horse) hair. . .' The mass of the Scots rural dwellers who clung to this primitivism are portrayed through the judgements of the improvers:

> they have neither activity or knowledge to cultivate their lands in any good manner. They languidly go on in the old beaten track and it never enters their thoughts that there is a better method.[10]

III

Shortly after the middle of the century, a number of works devoted more specifically to the history of agriculture and rural society appeared, the best known and probably most widely read being T. B. Franklin's *History of Scottish Farming* (1952); J. E. Handley's *Scottish Farming in the Eighteenth Century* (1953); and J. A. Symon's *Scottish Farming Past and Present* (1959). The evidence which appears in these works, and their authors' use of it betray little development from the sources, and historical perspective, adopted by Graham in the nineteenth century.

It has been pointed out that the periodisation of Scottish agrarian history reflected in such works, has tended to identify three phases. First, the period from the tenth century to the Reformation. Second, the period from the break-up of the monastic orders to the 1690s. And last, the eighteenth century and the 'agricultural revolution'.

The first of these periods is generally adjudged a fairly advanced phase largely on the evidence from the religious orders, while the modern age is considered to encompass the inception and progressive triumph of modern agriculture and the modern landscape. However, the historiographic treatment of the second period — the seventeenth century and the 'transitional' period at its end — is of particular interest.

Even in the simple narrative account of 'what happened', little attention was devoted to the seventeenth century:

> Agriculture in late sixteenth and seventeenth century Scotland

was largely ignored. . . An early history of Scottish agriculture
which directed ten chapters to the achievements of monastic
agriculture before leap-frogging to a panegyric on the
eighteenth century improvers dismissed the period in a
mere eight pages. A more recent history of Scottish farming
dealt summarily with the seventeenth century in a chapter
significantly entitled 'Before the Dawn'.[11]

This disinterest itself reflects that characteristic set of assumptions
about Scottish history which, in the last chapter, was traced in the
standard texts.

Amongst these notions, one in particular seems prior to all
others, seems quite fundamental. Once again this consists in a
Manichean projection of the pre- and post-Union Scottish world, a
contrast almost Stevensonian in its extremity and the suddenness of
its onset.

Scottish agriculture was conceived as passing through a 'centuries
old sleep' extending to the end of the seventeenth century which
'can be described as the dark period that precedes the dawn'.[12]
The comatose Scottish condition in this period is contrasted with
the lively dynamic of English husbandry.

The few changes acknowledged as originating before 1700 were
seen as occurring largely because of the Scots' experience of
England or the influence of the occasional English immigrant.
Indeed the inferiorist perspective extends to the regret that
this awkward country was not more thoroughly colonised by
'God's Englishman' in his efforts to civilise the 'dark corners' of
Britain:

> Had he lived longer, Cromwell, who was conscious of the
> backward state of Scottish agriculture, might have expedited
> developments. Commissioners were appointed in 1650 by
> the English Parliament to improve lands in Scotland but
> apparently nothing was done.[13]

What, then, flooded light upon the dark tracts of the Scottish
landscape? J. A. Symon's chapter on the subsequent period is
entitled 'The Dawn: 1700--1749', so one might surmise that the
years around the turn of the century constituted a period of
particular innovation, activity or general change. This notion is
quickly dispelled and we learn that there was in fact but a 'dismal
dawn'. (In proof of this there follows a sustained description of
the crop failures and poverty which occurred between 1693 and
1702 — though there is no suggestion that such agricultural
catastrophes might have been exceptional, as indeed they were,
in the seventeenth century).

But a miraculous change *was* at hand. The rural Scots, like Saul of Tarsus, were arrested on their unworthy, darkened way:

> The Union of Parliaments in 1707 was an event of the greatest importance to Scottish agriculture. On their journeys to and from London, Scottish members of Parliament were much impressed by improvements in farm practice in England. . .[14]

This sense of the near-incredible suddenness of the change and the crucial agency of the Union in bringing it about, is uniformly rehearsed in the other traditional histories. T. B. Franklin states unequivocally that a 'miracle' was performed in transforming Scotland from her condition prior to the Union to her prosperity of a century later. After giving short shrift to any consideration of seventeenth century developments, he identifies the cause of this transformation:

> The real agrarian revolution, involving the abolition of run-rig and the enclosure of the fields, had to wait until after the Union of Scotland and England in the year 1707.[15]

In this way of seeing Scottish history, emphasis is given to the progressive nature of *all* English people who were able to influence Scottish development.

Franklin has his 'Scottish Agricultural Revolution' initiated almost entirely through a remarkable piece of social engineering by a single English lady. After the Earl of Peterborough's daughter married Lord Huntly in 1706, she introduced English ploughmen, ploughs and habits of fallowing. But over the succeeding twenty years, Franklin tells us, she

> persuaded other proprietors to copy her example and was the first person who was effective in introducing any agricultural improvements into the country.[16]

It is interesting to note that the purposiveness of the English visitors is not related to their class: the reason they are as they are is entirely a function of their nationality. The common farmers brought to Scotland by the likes of the new Lady of Huntly are uniformly portrayed as stout, free yeomen, ingenious, progressive and hard-working.

The natives are seen in a very different light, though once again the descriptions are generic and applied across the social spectrum. Franklin portrays the lairds and their tenants as sunk in ignorance and poverty. The resistance of the tenantry to enclosure confirms them as 'superstitious' and uniformly lazy.

In his descriptions of the Scottish populace before the Union, J. A. Symon typically relies heavily on the impressions of English travellers. His conclusion from these accounts does not suggest a major effort of historical interpretation: 'Sloth, ignorance and poverty seemed then to be the dominant characteristics of the Scots'. And a little later 'Dirt, disease, sloth and narrowness of outlook' are described without qualification as typical of the Scots before the Dawn.

J. E. Handley, again largely on the basis of English travellers accounts, asserted that poverty in the Lowlands

> had developed in the Scottish peasant a spirit of apathy and listlessness which prevented him from seeking out ways and means to better his condition[17]

And, (despite quoting contrary evidence in a footnote) Handley accepts similar judgement on the Highlands:

> English travellers who visited the Highlands and the Hebrides in the eighteenth century commented on the general listlessness . . . and laziness of the peasantry.

The unrelieved and quasi-racial judgements of these travellers are repeatedly alluded to or quoted with no hint of an interpretive gloss. The typical judgement is reflected in the following passage from Wolfe's account, quoted uncritically by Handley:

> The soil is much the same for some space either north or south [of the Border], but the fences, enclosures, and agriculture are not at all alike. The English are clean and laborious, and the Scotch excessively lazy and dirty, though far short, indeed, of what we found at a greater distance from the borders.[18]

This tendency to 'see' the inhabitants of the Scottish rural landscape through the eyes of (mainly) English visitors and travellers extends to T. C. Smout's *History of the Scottish People*. Smout relies heavily, at times exclusively, on such descriptions (usually reproduced from Hume Brown's *Early Travellers in Scotland*) in portraying the domestic life of the populace. However he is careful to avoid simply reproducing these quasi-racial observations and too closely associating himself with such crudities. Smout's approach is, rather, to adopt a kind of social-anthropological standpoint which, even if he is not producing much actual evidence for the history, at least provides a useful pseudo-scientific cloak of 'objectivity' for the historian.

Thus, having assumed in the absence of evidence the volume of household goods of a typical seventeenth-century cottar, he observes:

> Such an almost complete absence of material goods may be found today in the peasant societies of underdeveloped

countries: we might guess that nearly half the Scots lived in
such a world.[19]

On the lower classes' attitude to dress, a similar comparison is
made: 'behind the poverty there was undoubtedly a wish to dress
as well as possible comparable to that in modern African or West
Indian societies where incomes are likewise at subsistence level and
housing squalid.' Again, the standard of diet is assessed as just above
'that of most very primitive economies of the present time'.

Some would no doubt consider that such a social-anthropological
comparison was entirely legitimate, and that resistance to it was a
paranoid reaction. This would be quite wrong. Smout's comparisons
function (in the present context) to reinforce a particular way of
seeing pre-assimilation Scottish society. The historian forms an
identification with the external (mainly English) observers of
Scottish society and invites the reader to join the group in
peering at these rural barbarians whose characteristics require
comparison with the 'primitive' tribes of the contemporary world.
In this way, the Scottish reader (and this is an extremely widely
read book) is detached, alienated from the pre-Union past. Smout
assures 'modern rural Scotsmen' that, on the evidence, they need
feel no sense of identity or continuity with their pre-Union
forebears:

> In many ways there are much greater similarities between the
> peasant culture of seventeenth century Scotland and those of
> the more backward tribes of Asia and Africa than between that
> culture and that of the modern rural Scotsmen who were their
> direct descendants.[20]

It is perhaps a measure of the inferiorism of the Scottish
'intelligentsia' that it has accepted so readily as a major
contribution to Scottish history a work which projects the
pre-Union Scottish people, probably the most literate and, in
the social and ethical governance of themselves, arguably the
most democratic in seventeenth-century Europe, as 'backward'
and 'primitive'.

To recap. Pre-Union Scotland is first conceived in terms of
barbarism, superstition and fanaticism (the charges are strikingly
reminiscent of those hurled at pre-colonial African cultures by
colonialist historiography). Scotland was 'for centuries held fast in
the grip of feudalism, superstition. . . religious discord, misrule and
fanatical adherence to outmoded customs and practices'.[21]

This is directly contrasted with the civilised mien of English
society. Subsequently the conception of the pre-Union Scottish rural
society and economy as 'backward' appears to permit, almost justify,

a contorted portrayal of the people who lived within it as ignorant aboriginals.

Indeed if we look a little more closely, the derogatory and dismissive judgements are discovered to extend to a whole variety of indigenous aspects of rural society and the landscape.

In what first appears an innocuous, descriptive passage on travellers' accommodation, Symon dismisses the tradition of Scottish baronial architecture as devoid of aesthetic and functional value:

> The tall, ungainly, corbel-stepped, gable-roof buildings which served [the lairds] as homes, though lacking in comfort, were to be preferred to the wretched hostelries.[22]

Equal revulsion is expressed for the domestic architecture and the very lay-out of the Scottish rural communities — at least where these can be seen to derive from pre-Union models. Discussing the village of Ormiston, the product of planning by the improver John Cockburn in the early eighteenth century, Symon observes:

> Today its wide street and its trees give it a spacious, dignified and attractive appearance which readily distinguishes it from so many of Scotland's ugly and badly planned villages.[23]

The Scottish baronial style is quite distinctive, a demonstrable and visible link with Scottish history as a particular history, an architectural reflection of Scottish society's turbulence, but also ambition in the 16th and 17th centuries. It has no significant equivalent in England where the early modern period had a quite different character.

Again, the scattered lay-out of many Scottish villages, which is indeed quite distinct from the more rectilinear, ordered and tightly-clustered English style and which Symon condemns as a failure in planning is, in reality, more likely a reflection of a different agricultural tradition. The bulk of Scottish agriculture was pastoral and it is generally recognised that pastoral agriculture gives rise to more dispersed farms than arable agriculture. These historians merely reproduce the judgement of the old English travellers in what they regarded as a barbarous land. They accept as the norm, the touchstone of the pleasing and picturesque, the tightly-nucleated English village, centering on its village green and sheltering in the lee of its big house. The tendency which begins to emerge is to divest of either functional or aesthetic value just those aspects of Scottish rural history which might normally be expected to confirm a sense of continuity with the past.

Indeed the entire effect of this historiographic enterprise seems precisely to ensure that those historical perspectives which might be said to contribute greatly, in normal circumstances, to the creation of a sense of collective identity and well-being in a culture are attenuated, and conceived as originating no earlier than the 1707 Dawn.

Once the poverty and barbarity of the pre-Union populace has been established, the bleakness and barrenness of the landscape demonstrated, the absurdity and ugliness of the villages emphasised, the worth of the great-buildings architecture dismissed, the entire 'way of seeing' the landscape becomes limited to and defined by the post-colonial period. By the mid-1960s J. B. Caird, writing about 'The Making of the Scottish Rural Landscape', dismissed from consideration any conception that the historical formation of the Scottish landscape had any relation to 'pre-colonial' times:

> The first impression of the visitor to Scotland must be of a rural landscape of geometrical lines, similar to the 'colonial landscapes' of the more recently settled lands. . . Scotland's rural landscape is in fact a landscape of 'revolution' rather than one of slow evolution, a landscape deliberately created mainly in the eighteenth and early nineteenth centuries.[24]

Here there begins to emerge the degree of pervasiveness and penetration of cultural colonialism within the thought-world of the Scottish educated class. The very topography of the land is invested with a repressive meaning. It cannot be conceived in terms of Scottish history and experience (which, it goes without saying, would have included exchanges with other, particularly adjacent, cultures). Whatever is conceived to be of value must be seen as due to the irruption of anglicised influence and improvement, a cast of landscape moulded by exogenous aid and conceptions. Ultimately it comes to have no previous, no other history.

IV

The impact of the historical attitudes and perspective projected by these historians of Scottish rural society is not of course limited to the rarefied world of the intelligentsia. As one would expect, these writers have had a considerable influence upon texts more popular and more widely influential than their own.

Consider, for example, the much-used *History of Scotland for Schools* by I. M. M. MacPhail, which was first published in 1956, and constantly reprinted through the 1960s and 1970s. It was designed for the senior history classes in the academic 'stream' of secondary schools as well as senior geography classes and 'most schemes of social studies'.

The first chapters — setting the scene for these Scottish pupils' introduction to the modern history of their culture — (not unnaturally) reproduce the academic historians' assumptions.

Indeed in the first sentence of the book it is emphasised that pre-Union Scottish agriculture,:

> was very backward in almost every respect . . .Visitors from England, where agriculture was more highly developed than in any other country of Europe except the Netherlands, were much impressed by the backwardness of the farming and the poverty of the people.[25]

The racial comparison drawn from Wolfe's account and also quoted by the 'professional' historians, portraying the English 'as clean and laborious, and the Scottish [as] excessively lazy and dirty' (see p. 38), is then reproduced in full. Thus characterising the unfortunate rural inhabitants, MacPhail proceeds with a familiar pattern of devalorisation of each aspect of pre-Union rural society in turn. These observations are based partly on Graham and the 20th century historians and through them, partly on the Improvers like Lord Kames or Ramsay of Ochtertyre, who are directly quoted.

Typical references by English travellers (again obviously drawn from the professional histories) establish the landscape as desolate and, inevitably, treeless. It is stressed that the rotation of crops in Scotland was backward compared to Europe, and specifically England, until 1700. The livestock was 'as poor and miserable as the crops'. The description of agricultural implements perpetuates the notion of the survival of the primitive and pre-civilised:

> The implements used in Scottish farming in the early eighteenth century differed little from those of pre-historic times . . . The harrows were made entirely of wood, and, according to Lord Kames, were 'more fit to raise laughter than to raise soil'.

Rural architecture, as we have seen elsewhere, is drawn into the general denigration. 'The castellated mansions (of the nobility) were gloomy without and gloomier still within, cold and damp in winter'. The lairds and substantial tenants' houses 'wore a look of decay' (Ramsay of Ochtertyre is quoted vilifying these), while the cottars' houses 'were mere hovels'.

These judgements culminate in a rather typical observation on the Scots from an English traveller:

The nastiness of the common people is really greater than can
be reported; their faces are coloured with smoke, their mouths
are wide, and their eyes are sunk.[26]

MacPhail goes on to explain that the remedies for all these ills
were initiated early in the eighteenth century by the improvers,
stimulated by English example.

V

There is another 'way of seeing' Scottish rural history. It has
been only briefly glimpsed up to now and much obscured by
the predominance of the works referred to so far. But it does
exist, and has received a boost from the recent expansion in the
publishing of historical works by Scottish-based publishing houses.

Caird's perception of the landscape — and all it implies — has
been and is, the generally held view. Yet an alternative view was
advanced, very persuasively, some forty years ago by H. G. Lebon
in articles published in the *Scottish Geographical Magazine*.

Concentrating on Ayrshire and Renfrewshire, Lebon acknowledged that on the replanned estates owned by the lairds
themselves, the landscape substantially changed its form. However
in the large swathes of country outside these estates, no such abrupt
metamorphosis occurred:

Here, the modern landscape grew out of the pre-Enclosure
lands, and concealed within the modern pattern of enclosures
are many more features of lay-out surviving unmodified from
before 1750. Of such the term *evolved* lay-out may be used
instead of *replanned*[27]

To illustrate this 'evolved lay-out', Lebon draws from the
Ordnance Survey map of Ayrshire two 'clusters' of modern
farms known collectively as 'Gabrochill' and 'Fullwood'. Anyone
possessed of a reasonable familiarity will recognise his description
of this type of landscape:

Winding roads of variable width, but generally narrow,
connect the two clusters and provide ways to neighbouring
farms and villages; irregular smaller enclosures, some planted,
envelope the farmhouses; the land around is divided into an
irregular mosaic or jig-saw of enclosures. Although there are
a few small plantings, systematic provision of shelter belts is
absent.

This is not the traditional histories' 'rectilinear landscape of
improvement': it is simply the Scottish landscape, a topographical
variation (like any other inhabited landscape on the Earth) on a

social theme, on the social theme of the particular culture which it ultimately sustains. Lebon proceeds, in a fascinating discussion, to demonstrate that these farm clusters have preserved their existence for at least 500 years (and perhaps nearer a millenium, into the Celtic era) and that their modern lay-out and characteristics are a product of evolved changes occurring throughout that period — of which the enclosures and planting of the eighteenth century constitute but one.

However Lebon's isolated challenge to the 'colonial landscape' could not be enough. It was not the concept of the 'colonial landscape' but the entire colonial historiography in this, as in all historical sectors, which required challenge. It is no surprise to learn that, in the words of a recent commentator, Lebon's original and challenging work 'strangely, has been ignored by many later writers'.

Twenty-five years after Lebon's efforts, Alexander Fenton attempted to modify the Manichean projection of the traditional histories, particularly their conception of the transformation effected by the Union.

In relation to the historical event itself, Fenton argued that the Union may simply have coincided with the beginnings of changes, particularly in arable land usage, which could have been expected in any case given the logic of indigenous development. Whether this is true or not, he much more crucially signalled the realisation that the historical accounts produced by the Scottish intelligentsia in the modern period have been written with a particular vision of Scottish history in mind:

> By the Union period, there were a variety of cultivating implement types in Scotland, whether drawn by animals or operated by the human hand or foot. These, though crude and clumsy as seen through the eyes of the 'improving' writers of the late eighteenth and nineteenth centuries, had nevertheless evolved over a long period of time to a sophisticated adaptation to their environmental conditions.[28]

But from this it may be realised that Fenton's emphasis on the continuities of rural development remained, like Lebon's, fairly particular; while his consciousness of the historiographic attitude of the improving and assimilationist writers of the previous two centuries, did not extend to those of our own time.

Recently, however, a work has appeared which offers a more comprehensive challenge to the traditional histories of Scottish rural society. In *Agriculture and Society in Seventeenth-Century Scotland*, Ian Whyte demonstrates a distinct awareness of the historiographic perspective which has been dominant in Scottish historical scholarship.

He observes that a principal characteristic has been to bewail the paucity and poverty of Scottish sources — a characteristic which extended to the agricultural historians. This assumption (which Whyte considers greatly exaggerated) created a justification, indeed a necessity of relying on secondary sources, and, particularly, the writings of the Improvers themselves. Thus, as in other areas of 'scholarship' relating to pre-Union Scotland, even quite recent studies are discovered to have relied upon the 'ideology' of the eighteenth-century assimilationists. This reliance naturally coloured the derivative histories:

> The tone of the Improvers when considering the traditional systems of agriculture in Scotland was invariably scathing . . . these men had a case to prove . . . they had a vested interest in drawing the most unfavourable contrasts between their practices and those of earlier generations. The whole ethos of the period favoured the uncritical condemnation of everything that had gone before.[29]

Reliance on such views has played a major part 'in the treatment of the seventeenth century as a backward period in agriculture'.

Whyte has no romantic or exaggerated notion of the global significance of seventeenth century Scotland. It was, he emphasises from the start, 'a small country located on the margins of Europe' with a 'limited and under-utilised resource base'. The significance of his own work is to consider the (pre-Union) rural history of this peripheral agriculture *as just that* and as a matter different from (though of course related to) the story of her larger southern neighbour.

While he has no intention to claim for this 'peripheral' nation a leading role in agrarian innovation, he does draw attention to accumulating evidence forcing historians to the conclusion that

> seventeenth-century Scottish agriculture was not as primitive and unchanging as had been believed. It even seemed that there might be a need to modify the traditional sharp contrast between the 'Agricultural Revolution' and the era of benighted ignorance which had supposedly preceded it.[30]

Whyte then takes this on, overturning in a carefully researched and not overstated way, the assertions and assumptions both of the previous histories and, in the process, of the Manichean historiography which the Scottish educated class has concocted from the views of the assimilationist Improvers.

In the realm of agricultural technique for instance, liming of the

soil was at this period one of the most advantageous innovations to
adopt and understand. H. G. Graham simply assumed that liming
of the soil was hardly practised in Scotland before 1730. Yet this
was absolutely untrue of the wide areas (the central belt, Fife,
Banffshire) with carboniferous strata containing limestone:

> there is plenty of evidence to indicate that the use of lime
> for improving soil fertility was known, and practised, over
> substantial areas of Scotland in the first half of the seventeenth
> century.[31]

As for developments in crop rotation, T. C. Smout has emphasised
that in England crop variation was practised quite often, 'even
turnips being included by enterprising tenants in the seventeenth
century'. Smout immediately drew a stark contrast with the Scottish
situation:

> In Scotland there is no evidence of such variation possibly
> because the range of crops was so much smaller — often only
> oats or bear (a primitive form of barley).[32]

Yet Whyte has demonstrated that quite different crops and more
complex rotations were widespread particularly in eastern Scotland:

> Taken overall, the evidence of the yields of these rotations
> suggests that the best of Scottish arable farming may have
> equalled the level of yields which were being obtained more
> generally in the better parts of England in the late seventeenth
> century, and may have surpassed those of considerable areas
> of continental Europe. The picture of arable farming in
> seventeenth-century Scotland is thus neither so uniform nor
> so bleak as has sometimes been made out . . . [33]

More generally, Whyte seeks to trace the development of the
improving 'attitude' itself. As we have seen, the traditional histories
portray the pre-Union Scots, peasant and laird alike, as sunk
in ignorance, a listless and backward crew. The impulsion to
improvement is projected as a purely eighteenth-century, post-
Union phenomenon, closely associated with the English or with
pro-assimilationist Scots. J A Symon magnified the role and
significance of John Cockburn of Ormiston, claiming he was
Scottish agriculture's 'first great improver'. The historian was
also concerned to note, in conjunction, that Cockburn had been
one of the members of the Scottish Parliament who 'had actively
assisted the negotiations leading to Union'. In practice, Whyte
observes, 'the climate of opinion had gradually moved *during the
(seventeenth) century*, towards one in which improvements were
gradually gaining greater approval. It is in this context that we
should consider some of the earliest efforts of eighteenth-century

Improvers . . . Cockburn of Ormiston's estate improvements from 1714 onwards, and those of Grant of Monymusk from 1716, for instance'.[34]

It might be added that Symon makes no mention of the appearance before the Union, and three decades before Cockburn began his work, of four Scottish publications urging agricultural improvement, two of them by Fletcher of Saltoun and Lord Belhaven who were among the most vociferous opponents of the incorporating Union and had (amongst others) conceived the possibility of a self-generated economic and spiritual regeneration of the Scots, motivated by a patriotic desire to better their society. Alas, such contributions were evidently too shadowy to be perceived by the traditional historians, peering through the half-light before The Dawn.

In his painstaking and thorough study, Whyte demonstrates that, throughout the seventeenth century, improvements were seen in a progressively more favourable light. The early eighteenth-century developments 'were not the first faltering, isolated ventures in agrarian change, but a direct continuation of the traditions which had been initiated during the seventeenth century. . .'

These discoveries dramatically alter the perspective brought to bear on the Union, which can no longer be projected as the miraculous *primum mobile* of improvements in Scottish agriculture, and of civilisation in Scottish rural society.

Writing in an age when the colonised self-image of the Scots was shaken to its foundations, and appeared likely to be overturned forever, Whyte is able to brush aside the painted veil of this traditional historiography. Its fictive characteristics can be perceived in high relief — the absurd, Dickensian dualities, the exaggerated Stevensonian contrasts, the retailing of scarcely credible causalities. And as this peculiar construction of the history of the land crumbles away, the derogatory projection of the people, too, begins to collapse: we come to realise that the descriptions of them are no more than caricatures, the historically insubstantial wraiths of a psychologically-interested, a venal historiography.

VI

These histories of rural society are no more than one instance of a wider historiographic perspective. And this historiographic perspective is itself but one projection of a certain way of knowing the world with which the Scottish intellectual establishment have provided Scottish 'civil society' as rationale and justification of an age-old enterprise.

It is not difficult to guess what this enterprise can be. To simplify the matter mightily, had this Scottish civil society a spokesman he might, on the basis of the historiography, be inclined to ask — 'How can we be blamed for our painful re-orientation of this people and their culture to exogenous modes? How can you say we have been unpatriotic or unconcerned? The assimilationist way the Improvers took, the way we have taken, is the way of modernity, of progress. *Look what it was like before*'.

If Scotland is to survive as a distinct culture it is essential that it generates other historical codes, an alternative historiographic explanation. Even within the limited scope of this essay we have seen that this historiography often functioned to devalorise or ignore just those historical aspects which might be expected to confirm the particularity of our history or to foster a sense of continuity with the pre-Union past. It is just such cultural artefacts and attitudes which are utilised by the thinkers and educators of other societies to develop a sense of confidence, and of historical 'perspective' — the sense of being at the still-developing end of a particular historical trajectory.

VII

It may be that the history and historiography of agriculture constitutes a source capable of casting a particularly revealing light upon structures of thought normally latent, normally so obvious as to be invisible. This latent thought-world might be conceived as the epistemological expression of powerful social and cultural groups, within what Immanual Wallerstein has called the 'core' societies of modern history — the quintessential attitudes of those who have dominated the Age of Development.

In the eighteenth century it has been pointed out that our modern metaphor of 'culture' was only beginning to form. But what was 'cultured' (cultivated) was already coming to signify what was progressive, rational, civilised. In the early decades of this age of development, the condition of arbori-culture, horti-culture and agri-culture were fundamental to such judgements, most of all in the 'core' societies and supremely in England where intensive capitalist agriculture had 'taken off'.

Hence the constant references of the English traveller-diarists to the absence of stands of timber; to the absence of laid-out gardens or planted parks around the country houses providing 'cultivated' prospects for the inhabitants; and most of all to the 'underdevelopment' of agricultural methods and technology. Already, with these visitors — but soon also with the improver-landlords and the writers and moralisers who served them — the process had begun whereby stages in the trajectory of English history would come to define for the succeeding centuries a typology of Progress, would become the waymarkers of the long march to civilisation and modernity.

The latent assumption in much of the agricultural history writing considered above is that any particular Scottish practice at any particular time should be assessed as to whether it indicated attainment of some stage in the history of English rural development — the evolutionary continuum against which the degree of progress attained should be measured. This led to anomalies which may be considered the ideological hiccups of a thought system whose taxonomy requires to comprehend and 'locate' the products of one cultural experience by holding them up to the patterns of *certain* others. Of the debates surrounding the widespread infield-outfield layout of Scottish farms, D. Turnock has observed:

> Arguments that see 'infield-outfield' at an early stage in an evolutionary sequence of field systems culminating in English open field patterns overlook the fact that rotation practices on the infield bring it into line with the supposedly more sophisticated 'three field system' of the English Midlands.

The infield-outfield system was perhaps the most characteristic element in traditional Scottish agrarian practice. Only in very recent times has research led to an emphasis on

> the dynamism of the infield-outfield system which has for too long been judged harshly for its inefficiency when in fact its only failing was to conflict with the ideal of the consolidated commercial unit that became the norm in the eighteenth century.[35]

This historiographic perspective has been adopted in many cultures, by no means only in Scotland. But sections of the Scottish land-owning and professional groups, together with the educators and writers associated with them were probably amongst the first to internalise a conception of civilisation diffused outward from certain central sources, by an Army of Light. The outriders of Civilisation entered Scotland through Galloway (and their horses could barely keep their footing on the ill-made tracks).

This conception pervades the histories considered in this essay.

And like many of the attitudes discovered in these histories, it is reflected in the historiography of the 'core' too. A recent volume in the 'Cambridge Studies in Historical Geography' series is devoted to *The Historical Geography of Scotland since 1707*. (The periodisation is familiar). Describing what are, indeed, some of the foundations of the historiography described above — the contributions from parish ministers which make up Sir John Sinclair's *Statistical Account of Scotland* — the author observes:

> The ministers supported the process of improvement almost without exception and most criticism is reserved for failure to make adequate progress . . . The accounts leave the reader in little doubt that the process of improvement was going on as they were writing. They present evidence of a characteristic diffusion process with backward areas being gradually drawn into the mainstrean of economic growth.[36]

It is understandable, probably it was inevitable, that the improvers and their historians would internalise this understanding of the past and reproduce the perspective in their own eighteenth century works. Doubtless it is also understandable that it should also appear unchallenged in the historiography of the core society, of the 'First Industrial Nation'. Yet we have also discovered it constantly recurring in nineteenth and twentieth-century Scottish historical work.

It may be that these effects derive not simply from the workings of metropolitan and colonialist ideologies, but from the pervasive influence of an entire 'episteme'. Within this thought-world the facts, the themes, the typologies and periodisation perceived within the history of the core cultures come to define, not only for themselves but for their satellite cultures, the very way of knowing what History is.

4

Scottish Nationalist, British Marxist
The Strange Case of Tom Nairn

In a series of remarkable and influential essays, Tom Nairn has attempted to theorise Scotland's history and cultural development, and on the basis of this work has come to support the nationalist cause. He has been seen, as a result, as one of the founders of 'a new and unsentimental intellectual nationalism' (Christopher Harvie). Nairn's work is certainly a unique contribution to analysis of the Scottish predicament, and one which cultural nationalists must come to terms with. We will try to do this here by considering three questions: what aspects of Nairn's position are of greatest value to nationalist theory? How does Nairn manage to wed nationalism to his Marxism? And what, precisely, is the nature of Nairn's own nationalism?

I

The work of a rigorous Marxist who has been converted to nationalism is clearly of particular significance for the Scottish left, and here, in the seventies, Nairn's influence was important. Given his impeccable credentials as a revolutionary theorist and *citoyen du monde*, his commitment to Scottish independence (which found practical political expression in his membership of the breakaway Scottish Labour Party) helped make the Scottish question appear more important — and nationalism more palatable — to many radical Scots who might otherwise have tended to dismiss Scottish nationalism as a parochial diversion, or, to recall that weary phrase, as 'tartan toryism'. Behind this commitment lies Nairn's questioning of the leftist shibboleth of internationalism.

Nairn has subjected the internationalist stance to damaging criticism on a number of levels. His main theoretical objection is that a peculiar myopia about historical development attaches to the internationalist's approach, an inability to recognise the nationalist character of modern history. Drawing an important distinction between *internationality*, the fact of economic interdependence, and *internationalism* as political sentiment or ideology, Nairn stresses that 'the overwhelmingly dominant political by-product of modern internationality is nationalism' — and not, as the internationalist is forever fantasising, internationalism. Balkanisation, not swelling 'higher unity' is the rule. But the internationalist's vision of proletarian solidarity hinders the proper perception of this elementary truth. Internationalism thus involves 'a crippling theoretical blindness'.

As far as political practice is concerned, commitment to world revolution can be a cop-out. The internationalist all too often ends up 'substituting the "international struggle" for doing anything next door'. Nairn notes, thirdly, that since the universalist too is rooted in a specific culture, in the world of messy particularism, closer examination of his views will invariably uncover chauvinist and xenophobe attitudes.[1]

This general critique of the 'internationalist' outlook is a logical extension of Nairn's lethal exposure of the jingoism and foreigner-hatred which gripped the British left at the time of Britain's entry into the EEC. The left was at one, as almost never before, united in forthright condemnation of the capitalist Common Market and its undemocratic institutions: Labour leaders, Tribunites, CP apparatchiki and Trotskyist sectaries were heard echoing the likes of the establishment constitutionalist Sir Ivor Jennings in defence of national sovereignty, the British Constitution, and the wisdom of British ways. The internationalism of the British left turned out, under pressure, to be a species of Great Britainism.

Nairn was one of the first to draw our attention to the fact that such great-power chauvinism, 'a mystical faith in the superiority of British society and the British constitution' is an essential part of the ethos of labourism.[2] This insight is as important and valid as ever, for Labour's Orwellian belief in the basic soundness and 'decency' of British institutions has survived into the 80s, as the briefest study of the party's thinking on Europe will confirm. Six Labour MEPs recently called for Britain's exit from the EEC in the following terms: 'What the Labour Party says is that our economic policies, our agricultural policies, our trade policies, should be decided *within our own democratic bodies* (our emphasis).'[3]

This touching faith in 'our own democratic bodies', and the assumption that foreigners have to make do with something less satisfactory, remain unaffected by the numerous demonstrations that Westminster represents, in the words of one critique, 'the most elitist, most secretive, most inwardly imperial and least reformable state in the capitalist world'.[4]

Chauvinism and cosy insularity co-exist in the Labour Party with an official rhetoric of class loyalty and international solidarity. Such hypocrisy, or 'idiot bad faith' as Nairn calls it, took on quite grotesque form in the seventies, when the Labour left's rabid opposition to devolution in Wales and Scotland, in the name of 'class before nation', went hand-in-hand with hostility to involvement in the EEC and calls for an alternative economic strategy which is brazenly (British) nationalist. About such 'internationalism', never such innocence again.

II

> Socialists must be internationalists even if their working classes are not; socialists must also understand the nationalism of the masses, but only in the way in which a doctor understands the weakness or the illness of his patient. Socialists should be aware of that nationalism, but, like nurses, they should wash their hands twenty times over whenever they approach an area of the Labour movement infected by it.[5]

If, in 1972, Nairn was able to see through 'internationalists', he seems still to have been a long way from any kind of acceptance of nationalism. Nowadays, however, he is himself willing to be numbered with the nationalists: in the 'Internationalism' essay, he states that he is writing 'from a nationalist point of view'. One would no longer expect him, then, to share Isaac Deutscher's conception of nationalism as a disease. But this raises a problem, given the traditional Marxist distrust of nationalist feelings and ideas and the doctrine of the primacy of class. As Leszeck Kolakowski reminds us, Marx 'envisaged the disappearance of the "national principle": so any tendency to cultivate national separateness and national culture must be a survival of capitalism'.[6] If Nairn no longer sees nationalism as a disease or deviation what remains of his Marxism?

In fact, even in the more recent essays collected in *The Break-Up of Britain*, Nairn frequently talks of the 'lunacy' and the 'symptoms' of nationalism.[7] He retains the physician's stance in his consideration of the Scottish 'case-history'. 'An aura of madness' surrounds Scottish nationalist ideology. Indeed, the Scottish nationalist seems for Nairn to be a doubly demented creature, since the result of union with England has been 'a characteristic series . . . of deformations and

"neuroses" '. Focussing on Scottish nationalism in 'Scotland and
Europe', he writes that nationalist consciousness 'should be treated
as a psychoanalyst does the outpourings of a patient. Where — as is
not infrequently the case with nationalism — the patient is a roaring
drunk into the bargain, even greater patience is called for.' So if
Nairn sees nationalism in general as insane and Scottish nationalism
as particularly neurotic, how has he come to identify himself with
the deranged?

For a proper understanding of Nairn's nationalist politics, some
acquaintance with the materialist theory of nationalism he presents
in *The Break-Up of Britain* is required. Nairn starts by insisting
that the meaning of nationalism is not to be found in the 'myths'
and 'rhetoric' dear to nationalists themselves. 'The subjectivity of
nationalism must itself be approached with the utmost effort of
objectivity', he warns sternly. The real, objective logic of nationalism
is connected with the unevenness of capitalist development, and the
relations which arise between ethnic communities at different stages
of economic advancement. Nationalism then has two distinct modes
(though they are 'impelled by the same underlying force', namely
the dialectic of development and underdevelopment): in one, what
might be referred to as classic nationalism, the sort which was
typical of nineteenth and early twentieth century Europe (for
example Poland, Catholic Ireland), a backward group mobilises
at the instigation of a middle class to resist the thrust of more
advanced regions; in the other, an advanced community feels
threatened by its less developed neighbours and attempts to shake
off ties which are conceived as impediments to further development
— Protestant Ulster, Catalonia and Israel furnish instances of this
variety. Contemporary Scottish nationalism, according to Nairn, also
seems to fit into this latter category. The SNP, he writes, 'perceives
a future of super-development based on North Sea oil resources, in
contrast to the declining industry of England'.

Insofar as the theory stresses the central role of the bourgeoisie
in the genesis of nationalism — 'nationalism was from the outset
a *bourgeois* phenomenon' — it does not seem to fit the Scottish
case particularly well, for no significant section of the industrial
or financial communities has come out in favour of independence.
Not even the discovery of oil has been enough to rouse the
bourgeoisie from their slumbers. As Nairn himself wrote in his
New Statesman report on the 1979 referendum, 'the bourgeoisie was
encamped solidly on the 'No' side'; it was 'the workers, students and
intellectuals, and some of the radicalisable lower-middle class' who
voted for a Scottish Assembly.[8]

But to return to Nairn's account: nationalism was the 'normal' reaction of small nations in nineteenth century Europe to the threat of active underdevelopment by the centres of economic progress. While the 'motor role' in nationalism is played by the middle class, the masses have to be enlisted to provide political support. The bourgeoisie 'have (usually) to get rid of an anachronistic ancien régime as well as to beat "progress" into a shape that suits their own needs and class ambitions. They can only attempt this by radical political and social mobilisation . . . the national or would-be national middle class is always compelled to "turn to the people".' This mobilisation, more precisely, is the 'formation of a militant, inter-class community rendered strongly (if mythically) aware of its own identity vis-a-vis the outside forces of domination'.

At this point a third social grouping takes the stage: the intellectuals. Artists, scholars, journalists and teachers function as — in Hobsbawm's phrase — the spokesmen of the middle class, the necessary link between the bourgeoisie and the masses, with the role of creators of the 'national identity', and the awareness of this identity, required by nationalist politics.

'Turning to the people', at the level of cultural production, is articulated as *volkism*. The intelligentsia take up the study of the history and habits of the people, rediscover vernacular speech forms and forgotten languages, and explore the simple virtues of peasant life. The cosmopolitanism and rationalism of the Enlightenment give way to a new respect for local traditions and a recognition of *gesundes Volksempfinden*. Nationalism's need to re-invent and re-animate the community, in other words, engenders cultural romanticism. As Nairn puts it, 'the politico-cultural necessities of nationalism . . . entail an intimate link between nationalist politics and romanticism'.

III

For Nairn, the great fact of modern Scottish history is the absence of an authentic nationalism precisely in that period — 1800–1920 — when the other small nations of Europe were struggling for and winning their independence. Rejecting 'voluntarist' and 'idealist' explanations of this absence (such as the treason of the intellectuals view offered by David Craig), Nairn is now in a position to put forward a materialist analysis. If no nationalist movement worthy of the name emerged, this must have been due to the fact that the main agents of nationalism — the middle classes — had in Scotland no material interest in the establishment of a separate state. 'The real participating factors of the nationalist response were not there'. But this of course immediately raises a further question: what was so different about the situation of the Scottish bourgeoisie?

Perhaps the clearest formulation of Nairn's answer to this question is to be found in his review article, 'Dr Jekyll's Case: Model or Warning?'9 Scotland, Nairn writes, represents one of the very few exceptions to the rule that 'capitalism perpetuates, or even intensifies, the relative deprivation of the periphery'. Unlike almost all the other small nations, Scotland was not confronted with the threat of forcible underdevelopment at the hands of a more powerful neighbour. On the contrary: Scotland was ushered by England into the rich men's club, and was able to reap the rewards of its industry as an imperial partner. This unbelievable stroke of historical luck was due to the fact that, before the modern era of nationalist sentiment, England — the world's dominant economic power with ample opportunity for further expansion — required a broader domestic productive system. 'The inclusion of the Lowland Scots . . . was the natural mode for England to expand its base', Nairn quotes Immanuel Wallerstein. Scotland — or at least Scotland below the Highland line — thus escaped the fate of other peripheral societies. It was, is, 'a freak by-product of European history'. However, Nairn continues, a heavy price was to be exacted in return for a place in the core: Scotland's freakish development would have the direst *cultural* consequences.

There was, then, in Scotland no 'real, material dilemma of underdevelopment', which is another way of saying that there was no need for nationalism, although, because of the country's long history as an independent state with a distinctive culture and the resilience of its native institutions, there was no lack of those national *differentiae* which, elsewhere, formed the raw materials out of which the intellectuals hammered a militant new 'national identity'. It follows that, since 'the Scottish bourgeoisie was not compelled to frame its own pseudo-organic "community" of culture, in order to channel popular energies behind its separate interest', the social setting which would have fostered romanticism was absent. Nineteenth-century Scotland, Nairn argues, produced neither a genuine nationalist movement nor a genuine Romanticism. Scott is clearly a crucial test here: to support his analysis Nairn invokes Lukacs' judgement that Scott was not a Romantic. Scott's aim in depicting Scotland's past is not (as authentic Romanticism would require) to revive it, to present it as a living tradition which should guide action in the present, but rather to bid this past a fond farewell. He was a 'valedictory realist', and thus the spokesman of a bourgeoisie who had, in real political terms, abandoned Scotland — however maudlin they might be about their native land in private life.

As a result of Scotland's exceptional status — a periphery not threatened with underdevelopment and so not requiring nationalism/romanticism — the Scottish intelligentsia was deprived of the normal function of 'marginal' intellectuals. Modernisation without nationalism meant that they were historically redundant. The consequence, Nairn goes on, was the more or less complete breakdown of 'high culture' in Scotland, that nineteenth-century cultural wasteland which has become a cliché of our standard intellectual histories.

'An anomalous historical situation could not engender normal culture'. Relentlessly pursuing the logic of his argument, Nairn goes on to describe modern Scottish culture as a long agony of mindlessness and kitsch. For it was not only high culture which was affected. Since the national culture had no head, no mind — that is, no high Romantic movement — popular culture was condemned to develop in a crazy fashion ('an especially mindless popular culture revolving in timeless circles'). Instead of the normal experience of nationalist culture, the Scots had only their 'remarkable assemblage of heterogeneous elements, neurotic double-binds, falsely honoured shades, and brainless vulgarity'. Vulgar tartanry became the central popular-cultural reality.

Scotland's 'sub-culture' (in Nairn's special sense of the phrase) had, as the reference to tartanry suggests, a nationalist, or rather 'sub-nationalist' character. The Scots were condemned to live in a world where nationalism was the norm without themselves — for the socio-economic reasons already described — being able to generate a nationalist ideology and a nationalist movement. Scottish society could only secrete a 'stunted, caricatural version' of nationalism — not nationalism, but gutless Scotchery. 'Sub-culture', 'sub-nationalism', a sub-nation.

'Scotland', Nairn comments, 'does appear as a sort of lunatic or deviant, in relation to normal development during the period in question. But one must never overlook the fact that it had found a comfortable — indeed extremely rewarding — asylum to live in, and consequently chosen to stay there'.

In the absence of any serious challenging of Nairn's work, his account of modern Scottish history and cultural development seems to be becoming authoritative, particularly for the sophisticated left. In the *Scotch Reels* volume, a prominent example of current cultural analysis, there is a quite uncritical deployment of Nairn's approach: 'Denied by history a place in the cadres of the forces of progress . . . Scottish artists and intellectuals . . . produced works in or about Scotland which were deformed and "pathological"'.[10]

IV

In Nairn's description of Scottish culture there are no shades or contours: *everything* stands condemned. It would be foolish, of course, to overlook the polemical intent behind these essays, but even when we discount the barbed presentation we are left with a remarkably bleak picture. Nairn shares with many Scottish intellectuals a deep aversion to everything native and local. It is this phenomenon, and the Scottish intelligentsia's internalisation of an Oxbridge view of Scottish culture, rather than the existence of Scottish kitsch, which, from a different perspective, require explanation. Exactly like the Canadian intelligentsia Dennis Lee has described[11], many of our intellectuals seem motivated by the fear of being considered, by metropolitans, to be like the rest of the natives, and consequently try to outdo each other in decrying the practices of those still sunk in their aboriginality. What such behaviour testifies to is cultural colonisation.

Even in terms of Marxist cultural theory, Nairn's total dismissal must surely be judged an inadequate response. For all its brilliance, this aspect of his work in the end falls into a mechanistic tradition, where culture straightforwardly functions to reinforce the existing social system, as Nairn finds nothing in the cultural landscape which is oppositional to the status quo, no traditions or practices which uphold values negating the dominant culture. It is a static, incomplete picture. A more 'dialectical' approach would acknowledge that culture must express a society steeped in contradiction, that a cultural whole devoid of all negativity is unthinkable.

Certainly nothing in Nairn's account, in which everything has the value of a tartan knick-knack, would allow us to describe it as nationalist in any accepted sense of the word. It is sometimes closer to the ravings of a Trevor-Roper than to what might be expected in literature of a nationalist bent. Nairn is openly contemptuous of cultural nationalist claims, referring, for instance, to 'nationalist paranoia about assimilation' to England. (The most obvious counter-argument to the view that Scotland has not been subjected to a *Gleichschaltung* is supplied by our thoroughly anglicised universities)

Here is a writer, one is almost tempted to say, whose profoundest reflexes are *anti-nationalist* rather than nationalist. But how, then, are we to explain Nairn's nationalist politics? Why, if Scotland is a vast asylum, would anyone who was himself *compos mentis* care — like Nairn — to walk arm-in-arm with the inmates?

The reader of *The Break-Up of Britain* looks in vain for traces of sympathy for Scottish traditions. An interesting aspect of Nairn's analysis which is relevant here is his treatment of the Scottish Enlightenment. The question of the origins of the Enlightenment — was it a Scottish or unScottish phenomenon? — is, he declares, a hoary dispute to which he does not want to contribute. But various comments and references disclose his attitude to the issue, and it is one which fits with the premises of metropolitan historiography: pre-Union Scotland dark, backward and dominated by religious obscurantism. The Enlightenment succeeded 'the age of witch-burning and feudal futility'; Scotland emerged 'from feudal and theological squalor', progressing from 'fortified castles and witch-burning to Edinburgh New Town and Adam Smith'. Scotland's Enlightenment thinkers were able to analyse the advancement of society from 'barbarism into refinement. . . because, obviously, they had actually experienced much of the startling process they were trying to describe'. Nairn's position here is not only naively progressivist (accepting uncritically the ideology of the eighteenth-century philosophers); it is also, for a *soi-disant* nationalist, a curious cave-in to the metropolitan view of Scotland. Here, it is perhaps worth quoting one of our sturdy empiricist historians, for an alternative perspective: 'Late seventeenth-century Scotland was not a by-word for ignorance, nor was there any break in the continuity of European influence on Scotland.'[12]

The reasoning behind Nairn's nationalist politics is presented most explicitly in 'Into Political Emergency', the 1981 post-script added to the second edition of *The Break-Up of Britain*. There, Nairn locates the significance of Scottish nationalism within the crisis facing the left — the British left, that is. 'Peripheral nationalism' (in Scotland and Wales) provided a way out for leftists trapped in an apparently stagnant political landscape. Given that the British state seemed immune to other threats, nationalism offered itself as the one force which could unite workers and intellectuals and mobilise a sufficiently large section of the population to constitute a fundamental challenge to the structures of the state. 'For over a generation, socialists had endured a wasting British world where no break gave relief. Overall decline and repeated economic crisis led to no rupture in the prevailing order'. Nationalism was an answer to 'the need of the post-war *British left* to discover . . . a way out and forward from its peculiar impasse' (our emphasis). It is deeply ironic that the renowned scourge of covert Great Britainism should himself be sporting underpants stamped with a Union jack.

Restated, *the meaning of Scottish nationalism for Nairn is as a moment in the development of British socialism.* His commitment to nationalism is pragmatic and conditional rather than principled. There is therefore no need for a *rapprochement* of Marxism and nationalism in his work: nationalism remains severely subordinated as a tactical option.

In 'Into Political Emergency', Nairn expresses with perfect frankness what was in any case always the basic position of the earlier writing. In the essay on Northern Ireland, for example, he writes that

> in a Britain dominated by an England in transition to socialism, it goes without saying that (eg) Welsh or Scottish separatism would become — at least in their present form — dubious or backward trends.

The essay on internationalism is a plea for socialists to take 'a more genuinely open and pragmatic approach towards nationalism', not a recipe for a new socialist philosophy which takes seriously questions of nationality, and the significance of nationalist (*cultural* nationalist) rebellion. Since, as Nairn writes in 'Internationalism', nationalism has become 'less of a threat to civilisation and reason themselves', the left would be foolish to pass over the chance of a ride on the beast's back now that progress under their own steam has become difficult.

V

A fundamental distinction — which cannot be drawn in terms of 'sentimental' as opposed to 'unsentimental' nationalism — must be made between those who see themselves fighting for a socialist future, and view nationalism as a tactical possibility within this struggle, and those who see the fight for a culture, a history, a people as an integral part of a socialist *politique*. The latter will define the purpose of nationalism in terms of the survival of the culture — and not, with Nairn (for whom Scottish culture is nugatory), in terms of the needs of the 'British left'.

Fighting for a culture means finding it a valuable inheritance. Cultural nationalists can only reject Nairn's evaluation of Scottish culture (and with it the assumption that cultures must follow some 'normal' trajectory). As far as what he calls 'social science, philosophy and general culture' are concerned, we would argue that the Scottish intellectual tradition did not die or gradually disappear after 1800. Under institutional pressure it was weakened and dispersed, for all that surviving and still capable of producing important figures. It is highly significant that, for example, French perspectives on Scottish intellectual history can differ radically from anglocentric viewpoints (one historian of ideas — Jean Pucelle — rating James Frederick Ferrier the greatest of nineteenth-century British philosophers).

Mention of the dispersal of the Scottish intellectual inheritance and the possibility of alternative ways of seeing Scottish culture suggests, further, that cultural nationalists will have a different view of the historical development of Scottish traditions. They will emphasise the adverse effects on Scottish cultural life of the adoption by many intellectuals of English modes. One result was the displacement of the country's philosophical approach from the centre of intellectual life. Another consequence is that English ways of interpreting Scottish culture and history have become, in Scotland too, hegemonal. Nairn's work, we have been arguing, is based on such readings, and thus exemplifies the adoption by Scottish intellectuals of metropolitan perspectives.

The task facing nationalists is to challenge this cultural power, to question its values and assumptions, to inquire into its operations; and, at the same time, to develop alternative codes for understanding ourselves and our past.

5

Philosophy and Autonomy

Although within the nationalist movement cultural issues have not yet been accorded the prominent position they merit, it is true that nationalists show some awareness that Scottish forms of life have been distorted or suppressed by the metropolitan culture, and that an effort of rescue and revival is required. The parameters of conventional cultural nationalism are well known, and need not be rehearsed in detail once more here. There are demands that the use of Gaelic and the different varieties of Scots be encouraged, and calls for more study in our schools and universities of Scottish literature. There is support for curricular changes which will give Scottish history a more central position. These concerns are reflected in the SNP manifesto section on education (we might note in passing that discussion of cultural matters comes at the end of the document): 'Gaelic should be encouraged as the teaching medium in Gaelic-speaking areas, and it should be available to pupils in secondary schools throughout Scotland . . . the process of anglicisation of the Scottish educational system whereby excessive emphasis is placed on English history, geography, literature, and habits must be reversed. . .'

Such proposals are important, but in the end seriously limited. They address the most obvious abuses and absurdities of an educational system which accepts the modes of an external culture, but ignore less evident, though no less important dimensions of our bondage to English cultural norms. The changes conventionally proposed would leave intact certain structures of the metropolitan culture, while failing to re-assert central aspects of Scottish culture.

Nationalists who take cultural questions seriously have so far had little to say about philosophy, and this is perhaps the most significant weakness of traditional cultural nationalism. The omission is surprising, for two reasons. First, one of the most powerful contributions to thinking on Scottish culture to appear in recent times draws attention to the emphasis placed on philosophy in the native academic tradition. In *The Democratic*

Intellect, George Davie argues that commitment to philosophical reasoning, or debate about 'first principles', was the defining feature of the higher education system in Scotland before the implantation of practices more congenial to English culture. Davie's contribution alone ought to have been enough to stimulate discussion about the role of philosophy.

The second reason is that over the last two decades or so the peculiarities of Anglo-American philosophy (which is the dominant tradition in Scottish universities too) have been the object of a great deal of analysis. Partly because of criticism of the established philosophical styles, questions about the nature of philosophy have again become a matter of controversy. Criticism of the triviality and conservatism of mainstream academic philosophy, analyses of its wider cultural significance, and debates about the function of philosophy should surely be of interest to those concerned with the development of Scottish culture.

What we would like to do here is extend the customary cultural problematic by taking up the issue of philosophical studies. The first part of the essay considers the main features of modern British philosophy and explores the meaning of this tradition as a cultural component. We then outline the views of some recent Scottish thinkers who have been hostile to the Oxbridge approach to philosophy.

I

Simplifying somewhat, we can say that twentieth-century British (or Anglo-American) philosophy has gravitated between two poles: logical positivism, and ordinary-language analysis. These two approaches have many common characteristics; most importantly, both involve, in comparison with other conceptions, a severe restriction of philosophy's scope and function.

The best-known representative of the positivist tradition is A. J. Ayer, for many years a professor at London University, then at Oxford, and the author of one of the classics of modern English thought, *Language, Truth and Logic*. This book, first published in 1936, is part of the staple diet of British philosophy students, and has had, arguably, more influence than any other on the direction of British philosophy in the last half-century.

Ayer's aim in *Language, Truth and Logic* is to delimit the range of propositions which can be considered meaningful or significant. Two groups of significant assertions are distinguished: those of

mathematics and formal logic, and those which are empirically
verifiable. Any discourse — and this is taken to cover most moral,
religious and political language — which cannot be accommodated
to either of these two classes is rejected as 'meaningless' or
'nonsensical' (these somewhat abusive terms would be modified
in some analyses in the positivist tradition to 'lacking in cognitive
meaning'). On the definition of empirical testability employed,
only the tautologies of logic and mathematics, simple statements
concerning matters of fact, and the propositions of natural science
are taken to possess cognitive significance. This was, of course — as
Ayer breezily admits in a conversation about his work — to reject
most of what philosophers in the past had done as 'nonsense', and
unworthy of serious attention:

> Anything which didn't fall into either of these two classes was
> regarded as metaphysical, and so as nonsensical. I took this to
> include a good deal of what had passed for philosophy in the
> history of the subject, and also all theology — all theological
> propositions, anyhow in so far as they affected to be about a
> transcendent being, were held to be meaningless.[2]

The application of Ayer's criteria of meaningfulness not only
damns most past philosophy; the work of contemporary philosophers
who operate in other traditions is also viewed as nonsense. This
intense parochialism is a marked feature of English philosophy.
Ayer's notorious dismissal of Heidegger in *Language, Truth and
Logic* is merely an extreme example of the way in which
twentieth-century English philosophers have tended to treat
Continental European philosophy. Philosophy in these other
traditions is either disqualified as incomprehensible, or else seen
as something other than philosophy. (In the light of such insularity
it is difficult to take seriously the solemn warnings periodically
pronounced by our unionist academics that independently-controlled
Scottish universities might turn into inward-looking and provincial
institutions.)

It is doubtful whether Ayer's theory of meaningful statements, if
applied with complete rigour, would leave any role for philosophy
whatsoever, or whether, indeed, the theory could avoid condemning
itself as nonsensical, since it belongs to neither of the two
classes of propositions it defines as significant. This problem
was acknowledged, but it was felt that a niche might be found
for the philosopher in the philosophy of science. Ayer states:

> I see the future of philosophy as lying after all where I put it
> at the end of *Language, Truth and Logic*, in its being the logic
> of science.[3]

Given the positivist dogma that natural-scientific knowledge represents the only significant knowledge of the world, it is natural that philosophers in this tradition have tended to see philosophy's only legitimate role in the articulation of the assumptions and procedures of natural scientists. The philosopher is then concerned, for example, to give a detailed account of the concept of 'empirical verifiability', and to define the criteria which make one scientific theory preferable to another. The latter task could be reformulated as the description of the conditions which make belief in a certain theory justifiable, and in fact Ayer goes so far as to define philosophy as the study of what constitutes good reason for belief:

> If I had to sum up philosophy in a sentence I'd say that philosophy is the theory of the form of the proposition 'p supports q'.[4]

Ayer's view of philosophy would not be accepted by members of the other main school in modern English thought, ordinary-language philosophy. But though it accepts that the philosopher can be concerned with more than issues in the logic of science, this tradition also involves a drastic restriction of the scope and nature of philosophy, in that philosophy is here conceived primarily as a form of linguistic inquiry.

The conception that philosophy is not directly concerned with the study of experiential reality, but rather with the study of language, is expressed in the distinction between 'first-' and 'second-order' inquiry. The first-order disciplines (physics, history, sociology and so forth) investigate the world, whereas philosophy, as a second-order discipline, is the analysis of concepts, or the meanings of terms. The notion that the philosopher interprets the world of experience is thus abandoned, and philosophy becomes a form of semantic investigation. It is hardly surprising that much philosophy in this tradition has tended to converge with certain areas of linguistics proper (Austin's work on speech acts, for example, has proved of great interest to linguists).

While not all ordinary-language philosophy is devoid of intellectual interest, the charge that it often degenerates into 'meticulous boredom' would be difficult to refute. For readers unfamiliar with this style of philosophy, the following passage from a standard textbook on Plato may convey something of its character, and help explain why this school is often said to have rendered philosophy trivial or banal. The authors are here concerned with the distinction between knowledge and belief:

> To say 'I know that such and such' is to say something logically different from 'I believe that such and such'. If I say 'I know

that two and two are four', in saying 'I know' I am committing myself to the position that what I know is true, and that I can't be wrong, i.e. that two and two cannot but be four. To put it more generally if I say 'I know that p' (where p is any proposition), then the statement 'I know that p' entails 'p is true'. Notice that it does not follow that p is in fact true. It may be that I have been mistaken in claiming to know that p, and thereby committing myself to the position that p is true: p may in fact be false. It is still true, however, that so far as I am concerned, by using the word 'know' I committed myself to the truth of p. If it turns out that p is in fact false, then my claim to knowledge was mistaken.[5]

A typical procedure in this school has been to examine 'what we mean by' or 'our concept of' this or that: for example, 'what do we mean by morality?' or 'what do we mean by freedom?' Paradoxically, in a movement characterised by a passionate concern with meaning, the terms 'we' and 'our' in this discourse were never subjected to analysis, and the fact that such terms are themselves problematic was overlooked. To proceed by inquiring into 'our concept of X' is to presuppose and imply a consensus in ethical, political, religious and cultural issues, a consensus which in reality does not exist. Of course, there may very well be basic agreement on most serious questions among linguistic philosophers (who are, typically, white, male, English and middle-class). But what *they* mean by something is not necessarily what others mean. (To begin with, *we* would want to contest *their* definition of philosophy.)

In this way, linguistic philosophy tends to mask the diversity of values and traditions and ideologies, and peddles the middle-class Englishman's value-system and view of the world as the only one. It is true that there is a 'common sense' or populist strain in the movement — related to a certain English pragmatism and distaste for theories invented by foreigners — but it is the common sense of a small, privileged group which is being defended.

When brought to bear on the traditional questions of philosophy, the techniques of ordinary-language analysis (the examination of 'our' concepts) produce responses which are almost laughably banal. In the no-nonsense spirit of Dr Johnson, the ordinary language philosopher dismisses the complicated systems of theorists by pointing to our normal, everyday use of terms. Is the world of sense-experience ultimately real, or just a reflection of some other dimension of reality? A confused question — replies the linguistic philosopher — which is based on a breach of the rules governing the use of the term 'real'. For it is simply part of the meaning of the term that it refers, in the expression 'the real world', to the ordinary, everyday world of sense-experience. Can human beings act freely, or is their behaviour always determined? Linguistic philosophers respond to this question by pointing to cases where 'we would say' that someone had acted freely — that is, where no moral or physical compulsion was involved. This appeal to everyday usage allows the philosopher to dismiss the most profound analyses of the ways behaviour may be influenced — but at the cost, clearly, of missing the point. No serious thinker who has written about freedom and determinism was concerned to deny that, in everyday speech, people are described as acting freely. The philosophical question is: how far is this common-sense attitude justified? Simply pointing to its existence is no answer to the question.

This flaw in the linguistic approach to philosophy was pointed out by Ernest Gellner in *Words and Things* (1959), a book which signalled the beginning of a revolt against the philosophical establishment within English universities. Gellner wrote:

> Linguistic Philosophy . . . consists of 'solving' philosophical problems by examining the actual nature of some concept, or the actual rules governing some kind of discourse, and then treating these *de facto* rules of language, its tacit definitions, as *de jure*, as valid answers to the question.[6]

To appeal to established discourses as a way of dealing with philosophical issues is to affirm the correctness of accepted notions. Philosophy, in this tradition, will always bring us back to 'our' common-sense view of the world. The world really is what it has always seemed, our obligations really are what we have always taken them to be. The inherent conservatism of the methodology has often been explicitly accepted by practitioners of linguistic philosophy. Anything we 'think up in our armchairs of an afternoon', J. L. Austin remarked, is unlikely to be as valuable as the wisdom of the ages inscribed in our everyday language. Ordinary language embodies experience and acumen of many generations of men' (to which feminists may want to reply that this is precisely why ordinary usage has to be critically examined, rather than slavishly adopted). The idea that philosophy always endorses a conceptual *status quo* is nowhere better expressed than in J. O. Wisdom's statement that 'philosophy begins and ends in platitude'.[7]

In support of this view of philosophy, appeal is often made to Wittgenstein's *Philosophical Investigations*, which has become a kind of holy scripture of the linguistic movement, with some of its remarks forming articles of faith for linguistic philosophers.

We may not advance any kind of theory . . . We must do away with all *explanation*, and description alone must take its place.

Philosophy may in no way interfere with the actual use of language: it can in the end only describe it. . . . It leaves everything as it is.[8]

It is important to note here, though, that while the linguistic school has made great use of Wittgenstein, Wittgenstein himself can hardly be considered a linguistic philosopher (any more than, in his early work, he can be seen as one of the positivists). In spirit, Wittgenstein and the typical twentieth-century English philosopher are worlds apart: Wittgenstein *lived* his philosophy, and scorned *Berufsphilosophie*.

It was on account of the conservatism involved in the suspicion of theory and the appeal to accepted usage as an authority that linguisticism came under attack from the New Left in the sixties and seventies. In *One-Dimensional Man*, Marcuse criticised linguistic philosophy's refusal to challenge existing discourses and its outlawing of conceptual innovations as 'odd' and 'puzzling'. Such features, he wrote, reveal the ideological import of the movement. Linguistic philosophy functions to reinforce 'established reality'.

It identifies as its chief concern the debunking of transcendent concepts; it proclaims as its frame of reference the common usage of words, the variety of prevailing behaviour. With these characteristics, it circumscribes its position in the philosophic tradition — namely, at the opposite pole from those modes of thought which elaborated their concepts in tension with, and even in contradiction to, the prevailing universe of discourse and behaviour.[9]

In both of the dominant philosophical traditions — logical positivism and ordinary language analysis — *philosophy becomes a specialism*, divorced from other forms of inquiry. The reduction of philosophy to the logic of science in the one, and to semantic analysis in the other, cuts if off from general social, political and moral issues, and excludes the conception that philosophy stands in a dynamic relation to conduct.

Modern British philosophy has had no great influence on philosophy and intellectual life outside the Anglo-Saxon world, a fact usually interpreted, by British philosophers, not as an indication of the oddity of their own work, but as confirmation of the backward nature of foreign customs. This attitude emerges clearly in the following passage, where the Oxford philosopher Geoffrey Warnock is replying to the question why such central

English figures as Austin and G. E. Moore should have received so little attention in Continental Europe:

> I'm inevitably rather guessing about this, because philosophy outside the English-speaking world is a field in which I'm not particularly well informed; but I'd be inclined to say that philosophers, at any rate in Continental Europe, have traditionally been looked to for what one might call comment on the human predicament — taking moral standpoints, and very often political standpoints; they've been expected to be casting a sage-like look over the present state of the world's political and moral goings-on, and for that matter its literary and artistic goings-on. Whereas both Austin and Moore regarded philosophy very much as an academic discipline, a subject with its own problems and its own standards, capable of proceeding quite independently, in a sense, of what was going on in the world at large. Both would have thought it quite inappropriate for a philosopher as such to weigh in on political problems, or moral problems, which conspicuously they didn't do; and I think this would seem acutely disappointing to somebody with what one might call the Continental image of what a philosopher should be like.[10]

In this passage, Warnock provides an excellent account of the content and tenor of modern British philosophy: an academic specialism, not concerned with political, moral or other 'goings-on'; cut off from 'the world at large', uninterested in 'the human predicament'; certainly not a matter of developing — *horribile dictu* — moral and political standpoints; smugly indifferent to its own narrowness and insularity.

The 1970s witnessed the emergence of the *Radical Philosophy* journal as the main voice of a growing opposition to the philosophical establishment. A major theme in the work of the Radical Philosophy movement has been the need to break out of the provincialism of British philosophical modes, and to stimulate interest in Continental thinkers and currents of thought long neglected by British intellectuals.

The antipathy of British philosophers to Continental European philosophy is no doubt one reason why many major philosophers remain largely unknown here, and why important intellectual currents often have a very belated effect on the British intellegentsia. As this suggests, the condition of British philosophy is not an unrelated, isolatable cultural phenomenon. It has contributed to the insularity and dullness of British intellectual life. Its hostility to theory, its empiricist reflex, its insistence on a specialist status echo and reinforce the characteristics of inquiry in other fields.

If British philosophy expresses the central tendencies of the intellectualism affirmed in the culture as a whole, then failure of cultural nationalists to take up the issue argues a serious blindness. This omission is all the more disturbing given the fact that established English modes are often accepted by Scottish intellectuals less critically than by the English themselves. For example, the Radical Philosophy movement, which seeks to displace the Oxford school, has had little impact in Scotland. Again, the departments of Scottish history have seemed determined to be out of touch with the intellectual movements of the age: witness that monument to drab empiricism, 'The Scottish Historical Review'.

Cultural nationalism, then, must also be about a transformation of philosophy. But, contrary perhaps to what has been implied, our models need not be Continental only. A number of recent Scottish thinkers, fortunately, have refused to bow to English approaches; and it is natural that we should look above all to them for guidance in the reconstruction of an autonomous intellectual culture.

II

In January 1984, *The Guardian* published a three-part report by Martin Walker on the state of British philosophy.[11] Given the ingrained hostility to ideas which characterises the British press, this was a welcome event. But regrettably — if predictably — no mention was made of Scottish traditions in philosophy. Walker described the uneasiness about 'Oxford philosophy' which has recently developed, but the reader was left with the impression that opposition in Britain to the analytic regime originated with Ernest Gellner and remained the prerogative of the English student movement of the late sixties, the *New Left Review* entourage, and the *Radical Philosophy* group, mainly a product of the English polytechnics. A less narrowly blinkered metropolitan perspective would have revealed quite different sources of opposition to the insularity and constrictions of modern English thought. Among Scots, there has always been hostility to positivism and linguisticism, and it has been expressed, not by marginal figures, but by leading academics.

In the work of John Anderson, for instance, the notion of philosophy as a specialism and the conception that it has a descriptive function (describing scientific procedure, or language usage), are strongly attacked. Philosophy, he wrote, occupies 'a central place in any cultural system,' and its role is not description, but criticism: criticism of the orthodox and fashionable ideologies, beliefs and values of the age. This emphasis exists too of course in the traditions of Continental philosophy, and Anderson's approach recalls Horkheimer's definition that *die wahre gesellschaftliche Funktion der Philosophie liegt in der Kritik des Bestehenden* (the true social function of philosophy lies in criticism of the actually existing world). The philosopher wars with complacency, is committed — as Kamenka glosses Anderson's view — to a life of 'permanent protest, criticism and self-criticism. . .' Anderson's lack of sympathy with mainstream British philosophy was quite explicit: 'technical exercises. . .now pre-empt the field'.

Anderson saw the displacement of critical philosophy by 'technical exercises' as part of the century's 'surrender to science'. Here he was voicing a common Scottish view. Indeed, the main developments in twentieth-century Scottish thought can perhaps best be approached as critical responses to the intellectual dominance of natural science and the advance of philosophical currents which appear to underwrite those attitudes conveniently referred to as 'the scientific worldview'. Philosophers in England, on the other hand, have taken the hegemony of science for granted. To quote one of the texts which has been most influential in twentieth-century English thought: 'The right method of philosophy would be this. To say nothing except what can be said, i.e. the propositions of natural science. . .' [12]

Scottish thinkers have been sceptical of natural science not in the sense of being anti-scientific or irrationalist, but in arguing that science is only one mode of human cognition among others. The distinction between philosophies which accept the restriction of the concept of knowledge to knowledge of natural fact and those which interpret knowledge in a much wider sense is one we meet time and again in the works of Scottish philosophers. The Glasgow professor C.A. Campbell, for instance, in his Gifford lectures of the mid 1950s draws attention to 'a very real divide between those who understand by 'experience' merely sensory experience, and those who believe that experience as a source of evidence is far richer than is allowed for by its arbitrary limitation to the sensory.'[13] This tradition stresses the need to assert and explore our other ways of knowing the world, for example the various dimensions of moral and religious experience.

The Hegel scholar T.M.Knox analysed the connection between orthodox British philosophy and the triumph of scientism in a highly interesting article called 'Two Conceptions of Philosophy', published in 1961[14]. Knox was concerned to criticise the approach of 'the dominant group of contemporary English philosophers,' and to indicate an alternative view of philosophy. He begins by raising doubts about the revolutionary nature of the linguistic method, which is, he think merely 'English empiricism' in a new guise. He confesses to finding the debates of linguistic philosophers 'intensely uninteresting'. 'The questions they discuss so enthusiastically are questions which, in the main, do not arise for me at all'. On the other hand, the methods they employ seem ill-equipped to deal with genuine philosophical problems, as opposed to 'puzzles': a question such as 'what is the chief end of man?' cannot be settled by an appeal to usage.

The root of the problem with contemporary English philosophy, Knox argues, is its acceptance of the dogma that our knowledge of the world is exhausted in natural scientific knowledge. Linguistic philosophers hold that 'science, and science alone, deals with fact.' But this abandonment of all experience beyond the sensory means that almost everything which is of importance is excluded from philosophy. English philosophers neglect the human world, rejecting all those levels of reality — our experience of others, of our own inner life, of morality, of beauty, of God — which are not amenable to scientific investigation, and they find their only vacation in the analysis of linguistic usage. (Or rather, he notes — hinting at an element of chauvinism — in the analysis of English usage, 'as if English were the only language'.) 'We are to ask, according to the linguisticists, 'not what goodness is, or truth, or beauty, but how these words are used.' Knox rejects this conception of the philosopher's role. A philosopher's answer to the question 'what is justice?', as distinct from a lexicographer's, is not an account of the use of the word 'justice': 'his concern *qua* philosopher is with justice, i.e. with an objective fact which also has its subjective side in experience and so with a fact of a kind outside the purview of physical science.'

The error in the linguistic approach is, precisely, that it excludes subjectivity. Philosophy's task, properly understood, is to explore 'the total experience of subject knowing object'. It is the expression of this personal experience: 'philosophy is always personal'; 'it is not wholly unreasonable to describe philosophy as self-knowledge'. We should not then speak of (impersonal) 'problems of philosophy', but always of a philosopher's problems. Knox goes on to criticise the kind of philosophical scholarship, typical of the analytic tradition, which abstracts a work from its concrete personal and historical setting and treats it 'as if it were not a work of literature but a series of mathematical steps'.

(Students of the recent history of philosophy in Britain will observe that Knox's critique of linguisticism parallels in many ways the arguments made fashionable by New Left Review critics and the Radical Philosophy movement in the later 1960s and early 1970s; and it is interesting to note Knox's critique receiving belated recognition in Mestavarios' recent comments on modern British philosophy.)

A further illustration of this kind of position is provided by H.J. Paton's Gifford lectures of 1950-1, *The Modern Predicament*. (Paton was professer at Glasgow, then Oxford, and a distinguished Kant scholar.) Science, Paton writes, is concerned 'only with certain aspects of reality'. It excludes such other fields as morality: 'what remains clear is that it has, and can have, no concern with with judgements of value or judgements of what ought to be: it can treat these only as emotive utterances or psychological events. Science seeks to be objective — to concern itself solely with objects and to eliminate all merely personal points of view. . ' For Paton, critical philosophy could not turn away from other forms of human experience, or from the point of view of the person as a subject and an agent. But the 'arid empiricism' he perceived as the prevailing trend in British philosophy seemed unlikely to develop in the directions he desired.

Paton's work focuses on the ethical consequences of the triumph of the scientific worldview. For it was his particular concern that the overblown role now accorded to science and scientific reasoning was threatening the claims of a less narrow conception of reason to demonstrate the possibility of fundamental moral principles: 'it is a serious matter, both for the individual and society, if men are to be told that there can be no objective moral principles — because these are not the same as scientific generalisations.' [16] Paton's attempt to elucidate and defend the Kantian ethic of respect for persons was intended, he writes, to counter the undermining of the moral life which the spread of the scientific *Weltanschauung* entailed, 'in these days when the pillars of European society are shaken, and when we are assailed on every side by prophets of unreason for whom moral splendour is so much illusion. . .'[17]

John Macmurray, professor of philosophy at Edinburgh from 1944 to 1960, was another critic of the analytic tradition, its obeisance to science and failure to engage with issues of broad human significance. 'The claims of philosophy have been steadily reduced,' he wrote , 'until, in contemporary positivism, it has shrunk to a mere shadow of itself,' seeking employment as a 'cleaner-up' for science.[18] Macmurray took the view that it was the philosopher's task to address the great social and cultural questions of the age — as he himself did, in his work on Marxism and 'the crisis of the personal'. For him philosophy was 'the attempt to understand the meaning of human experience in the world'. Thus it should not be a specialism, and where it becomes a narrow academic discipline it ceases to be interesting. This vision of philosophy as a form of 'democratic intellectualism' was expressed in the radio talks he gave in the early 1930s.

> Philosophy goes dry and barren and meaningless when most people are not interested in it. It really comes to life when the mass of men begin to feel the need of it, to call for it, to support the struggling intelligence of the philosopher with sympathy, with the sense that what he does matters to men.[19]

Scottish hostility to the subordination of philosophy to science or semantics could be fierce, as in the frank personal retrospect appended to his final book by John Baillie, philosopher and theologian, and professor of Divinity at Edinburgh from 1934 to 1956. Here Baillie returns to the objections, which feature throughout his work, to analyticism, 'the school of logical and conceptual analysis which has recently dominated the philosophical thinking of Oxford and Cambridge'. He has, he writes, learned from and made concessions to the teaching of the movement, but 'when I am asked to swallow it whole, I become angry, and the more of the recent books I read by its representatives, the angrier I become.' The analytic movement is theoretically misguided in restricting the concepts of knowledge and reason to scientific knowledge and scientific reasoning. But Baillie's disagreement is not merely intellectual. 'Reductive naturalism', by devalorising the world of ethics and interpersonal experience, tends to have a disastrous effect on the attitudes of those who come under its influence.

> Nor do I speak here of their morals in any ordinary sense, for we are all miserable sinners, but of a certain painful restriction of outlook, of interest, of understanding and of sympathy which seems to leave them as very incomplete human beings. . . I confess that in my heart of hearts my impatience with them knows no bounds.[20]

Like Paton, Baillie was especially concerned about the ethical subjectivism which the analytic school had done so much to propagate. (By subjectivism we mean here the kind of view expressed by Bertrand Russell when he wrote, in *Religion and Science*, that 'if two men differ about values, there is not a

disagreement as to any kind of truth, but a difference of taste. . .')
Baillie's response was to urge a broader form of empiricism which
recognises all the dimensions of human experience (including the
moral and religious), not only those admitted by the positivists.

From one perspective, Baillie will be seen as the defender of a
conservative common sensism, hopelessly out of touch with the
important philosophical developments of the twentieth-century. But
his concerns emerge in a different light if we take a broader view and
consider intellectual movements in continental Europe. For there
are distinct parallels between the thinking of Baillie (and a number
of other Scottish theorists) and, for instance, the German traditions
of resistance to positivism, or the triumph of 'calculative reasoning'
(Heidegger) and 'the suppression of the ethical as such' (Habermas).

Turning to more recent thinkers, we should first mention John
Macquarrie, in whose work we also find criticism of the narrow
range of analytic philosophy and its failure to attend to the full
spectrum of human experience. Instead of a 'philosophy of the
object' (science, or language) Macquarrie urges an examination
of the parameters of human subjectivity. Macquarrie finds in
existentialist schools a more fruitful and important tradition than
analyticism. Echoing the position of Campbell (his former teacher),
Baillie and Macmurray, Macquarrie supports the existentialist
insistence that 'there are many rich strands in human existence
that ought not to be ignored or downgraded just because they
cannot be fitted into the logic of mathematics or of the empirical
sciences. This is not to condemn logic or to embark on intellectual
anarchy. At its best, it is an attempt to develop a logic of persons in
addition to our logic of things.'[21]

Finally, in this outline of the broadly-based Scottish resistance
to modern Anglo-American philosophy, let us consider the position
of Alasdair MacIntyre, who has produced a body of work of
remarkable scope and import. While never dismissive of analytic
techniques, MacIntyre has constantly criticised the limited vision,
atomism and tendency to triviality displayed in the work of many
contemporary Anglophone philosophers. His writing has always
been informed by a passion and concern which are alien to
the spirit of Oxbridge analyticism. He has been determined to
pursue the large issues and to engage with the major contemporary
ideologies, as is demonstated in *Marxism and Christianity*, *Marcuse*
and *Against the Self-Images of the Age*. In *A Short History of
Ethics* and *After Virtue* he expresses the conviction that there is
an interplay between ethical theory and social formations such
that moral philosophy can never be viewed as a form of inquiry

relevant only to specialists. MacIntyre's work demonstrates that philosophy, without any abandonment of rigour, can still be the attempt to say something important and profoundly relevant to all our lives — rather than, in his own words, merely the deployment of a professional idiom and technique.

In his most recent work, *Whose Justice? Whose Rationality?*, MacIntyre expresses his opposition to the specialisation of philosophy in words which echo the position of the other thinkers we have mentioned here:

> the conception of philosophy as essentially a semitechnical, quasi-scientific, autonomous enquiry to be conducted by professionalised specialists is in the end barren. There is indeed in philosophy a large and legitimate place for technicality but only insofar as it serves the ends of a type of enquiry in which what is at stake is of crucial importance to everyone and not only to academic philosphers. The attempted professionalisation of serious and systematic thinking has had a disastrous effect upon our culture.

In MacIntyre — as in Anderson, Macmurray, Baillie et al — philosophy is bound up with Kulturkritik. MacIntyre's moral theory is an attempt to combat the post-Christian, post-marxist atomism which characterises contemporary intellectual discourses and ways of living, and to counter 'the spirit of an age in which the future is always conceived of as a larger edition of the present'.[23]

But having indicated the deep Scottish opposition to the culture of Anglo-American philosophy, it is now time to turn to the positive contributions to contemporary intellectual debate made by thinkers who have emerged from Scotland in the recent period.

6

Philosophical Education

Any nationalist discussion of educational issues must begin with a consideration of George Davie's *Democratic Intellect*. And it is perhaps fitting that we should start our treatment of the book by pointing out that it anticipates one of the main themes of the present essays: the Scottish intelligentsia's dependence on English cultural modes. 'Increasingly', Davie writes,

> the only points of view about education or culture which are taken seriously by responsible Scots are those which are reckoned respectable and fashionable over the border.[1]

There is, he says, as a result, very little knowledge of or interest in native academic traditions. Davie no doubt hoped that his book (first published in 1961) would help to re-awaken interest in Scotland's independent intellectual history, and thus contribute to the achievement of a greater degree of cultural autonomy. Unfortunately, however, *The Democratic Intellect* seems to be more often discussed than actually read, and the standard debates about the book conducted by those who control discourse on Scotland have tended to cloud rather than to clarify Davie's concerns (these debates typically centre on the question of how open Scotland's education system was to all social classes and thus divert interest from *cultural* to *sociological* issues).

I

Some nationalists seem to have the impression that *The Democratic Intellect* is a hymn of praise to our present-day education system — on account of its 'democratic' character, or 'generalist' approach, or both. So it is important to recall that Davie is describing the *decline* of the native intellectual tradition, and that he sees the relics of this tradition — such as the Scottish ordinary or general degree, often cited approvingly in the context of Scottish generalism — as broken-down institutions rather than reasons for self-congratulation. The general degree, according to Davie, was a sop to Scottish pride at the time of the changes (recommended by the 1889 Universities Commission) which signalled the last major phase in the struggle to bring Scotland's higher-education practices into harmony with those south of the border. It ensured the survival, despite these changes, of the Scottish tradition — but survival in 'fossilised form':

> The great significance of the 1889 Commission seems to me to consist in its strong presentiment that the Scottish heritage could much more easily be retained in a fossilised, static form, incapable of giving much trouble, than in a developing condition in which it might — from the British point of view — prove embarrassingly alive. Accordingly, the Commission's prime contribution to education was to suggest the introduction of a dual system which ordained the coexistence, side by side in the same institutions, of a Scottish principle which represented the national inheritance but which was to have little or no future, and of an English principle to which, in spite of its alien character, the future was to belong.[2]

From this time on the brighter and more ambitious students would follow the English principle, while the general degree became an option for the less gifted (a disastrous recipe, of course, for the native intellectual tradition).

> A training in the old and general style (or at least an imitation of it) was still available for those students destined for local and provincial work as ministers or school teachers or minor officials; but those of their fellows aspiring to swell the growing ranks of organisers and specialists required for the new Imperial Britain were relieved of the burden of doing compulsory philosophy and, instead, were given a narrower type of training which left them intellectually indistinguishable, or almost so, from the southern product — at any rate provided that, after taking their Scottish degree, they spent a year or two at Oxford or Cambridge acquiring the necessary polish.[3]

This was a compromise which seemed to let the Scots have their cake and eat it: the local tradition would survive, but at the same time the way was cleared for the more dynamic students to prepare themselves for careers in England and the Empire. This meant, however, that the native tradition was drained of talent and vitality, and thus unlikely to foster significant intellectual achievement.

> One may suspect that both the self-interest and the sentimentalism of the Scots were gratified by a compromise which seemed to seal off from the movements of the modern world and to

preserve in a frozen form a vestige of their traditional intellectuality, at any rate for the unadventurous types, and which, at the same time, was to allow the more energetic individuals to devote their whole attention to their specialist careers and to free them from all feeling of responsibility towards their nation's cultural heritage.[4]

Davie's book is essentially a description of the long nineteenth-century *Kulturkampf* in Scotland, which pitted those who wished to see education evolve in the spirit of local traditions against those who favoured the adoption in Scotland of the specialising and untheoretical approaches to education favoured in England. This was more than just a quarrel about academic curricula: at stake — to put the matter in grand terms — was the future of Scottish civilisation: 'What was being decided by the struggle was the fate of the distinctive sort of society developed by the Scots.'[5]

Davie rescues this neglected dimension of Scottish history, and at the same time presents us with an account of the distinctive nature of Scottish education and educational philosophy before the dilution and distortion of the native tradition caused by the nineteenth-century reforms.

What, then, was the main feature of the traditional Scottish system? The term 'generalism' is often used here, but it is too ambiguous. The *differentia* of Scottish higher education, Davie maintains, was the central place accorded to philosophy. The ideal was that specialisation should follow a broader course in which philosophy played a key part. This broader course, or 'general education', was 'distinguished from other countries by the prominence given to the teaching of philosophy'.[6] Philosophy occupied 'a commanding position in the higher education system'.[7]

This being the case, the future of the Scottish academic tradition turned on the fate of the compulsory philosophy class in the country's universities: the crucial educational issue of the nineteenth century was centred on the question of whether or not to keep alive the tradition of the *classe de philosophie*.[8] The nation's philosophical education involved not only an introduction to metaphysics, epistemology and ethics, but also more general reflection on human nature and society. John Stevenson, Professor of Logic at Edinburgh in the mid-eighteenth century, had his students write on subjects like 'the nature and origin of poetry', 'Roman education', and 'the difference between mathematical reasoning and philosophy'. Davie mentions as another example the logic class conducted by George Jardine, Professor of Logic at Glasgow from 1774 to 1827:

the themes set are often concerned less with pure philosophy than with the problem of applying first or philosophical principles to literary, historical, linguistic and economic subjects. Thus Jardine speaks of the following as stock subjects for essays: What is the ground of distinction between the liberal and the mechanical arts? — How may the Iliad and the Odyssey be compared and on what principle is the preference determined? — What was the state of the Highlands of Scotland as indicated by the poems of Ossian?. . . What are the proofs by which Horne Tooke confirms his theory of the origin of prepositions and conjunctions in the English language? — What were the causes which produced an absolute government at Rome under Augustus? . . .The essay writers were always expected to bring the subject of discussion back to first principles. For example, in dealing with the question of how the Empire started at Rome, it would be necessary to refer back to some general theory of the conditions (economic, sociological, etc) in which authoritarianism succeeds constitutionalism. . .[9]

This commitment to theoretical reasoning, Davie argues, also characterised study in the other disciplines. Thus, in medicine, first principles were not neglected in favour of practical issues, a situation illustrated by the fact that

the chief interest of a man like Cullen was in finding a general theory of disease which would connect up with speculation about the nature of life, and its relations to mind and matter.[10]

The Scottish emphasis on 'enlarged investigation' was evident in Latin and Greek too; mastery of grammar and detailed textual knowledge were considered less important than reflection on more fundamental issues like the nature of life in the ancient world. This approach was expressed by the Humanities professor John Stuart Blackie in the following way:

The question whether the conjunction *ut* in certain cases should be followed by the perfect or imperfective subjunctive seemed not of the slightest significance in reference to the main end of classical education. What I wanted was, through Latin, to awaken wide sympathies and to enlarge the field of vision.[11]

The Scottish bent for argument about first principles meant that what Davie calls 'the common sense of subjects' was put before questions of detail. It is in this sense that Davie uses the idea of 'democratic intellectualism' to characterise the Scottish mind. For in discussing these general, fundamental issues — like the nature of aesthetic experience, the aims of education, or the value of a particular technology — professors and students, specialists and laity can meet on more or less equal terms, and the unlearned no less than the learned have a contribution to make.

Davie relates how the Scottish approach to education came under attack in the nineteenth century, and describes the efforts of those who defended it and worked for changes which would not break with the basic principles of the nation's intellectual heritage.

The Scottish system first came under scrutiny with the Scottish Universities Commission of 1826. Reformers criticised the metaphysical bias of the native approach, and urged that greater emphasis should be placed on exact knowledge. In his evidence to the Commission, Francis Jeffrey acknowledged the force of criticism that Scottish students tended to be weak on matters of detail, but he rejected the idea that there was anything fundamentally wrong with the system. Its great strength lay in its encouragement of passion for intellectual argument: 'Young men in the humanity class will insist on discussing all the debatable points in history, politics, physics, metaphysics, and everything'.[12] A majority on the Commission were inclined to accept the more negative assessments, however, noting that the students were thrown much too early into 'the abysses of ancient and modern metaphysics, before they have had time to master the classics'. The memory did not receive enough training, and there was a tendency for students to lapse into dilettantism: 'the student . . . is in danger of passing out a sciolist and a smatterer in everything'.[13]

The poor performance of Scottish students in the Indian Civil Service examinations (which stressed detailed knowledge in Greek and algebra) is seen by Davie as a major cause of the second educational crisis, in the 1850s. There was heated debate on the future of the country's universities, controversy which featured, on the one side, anglicisers like J C Shairp (later Principal of St Andrews), and, on the other, traditionalists like Professor James Lorimer, who, although no less keen on change, were not prepared to accept that the basic principles of the national tradition had been rendered obsolete.

In Shairp's view, Scottish students received too much metaphysics and not enough facts:

> of a loose discursive intelligence which can deal readily with things in general there is abundance; of power to write plausibly on almost any subject in a fluent semi-metaphysical, semi-rhetorical way there is no lack; but it is when brought to book that our weakness comes out, when not crude views of things in general are called for, but accurate knowledge of

some things in particular, combined with some accuracy of scholarship and some definite historical knowledge, it is here that our students fail.[14]

Shairp stood for a down-to-earth, empiricist intellectualism which scorned the 'wordy theories' and 'spun-out abstractions' the Scots seemed to find appealing.

What more pitiable then to see a youth, who, with no previous training to fit him for abstract thought, has just quickness enough to pick up the chief technical terms, prating glibly about 'the ego and the non-ego', 'the relative and the absolute', and fancying that such gibberish as this will really solve the deep things of thought.[15]

Lorimer, for the traditionalists, defended the idea of a basic, compulsory university course which was broad and philosophical. Such an arrangement was integral to the uniqueness of Scottish culture: Lorimer was intent, in his own words, on 'perpetuating the distinctive intellectual character of the Scottish people', and on preserving 'a school of thought which is peculiarly Scotch'.[16] He urged the setting-up of postgraduate research schools which would cater for the more gifted who wished to specialise, at around the age of twenty — but specialisation would only be possible after the student had finished a general first degree.

Lorimer seems to have believed that Scottish education had reached a crossroads: unless changes were made which respected the basic character and principles of the native tradition, the universities would be assimilated to the English system, and Scottish culture as a whole gradually provincialised. Edinburgh would be, either, on the basis of the reforms Lorimer envisaged, a *Kulturstadt*, the centre of an autonomous national culture, or else a mere cultural province aping the styles fashionable in the south. Westminister, unsurprisingly, showed little interest in making funds available for Lorimer's unEnglish scheme for the universities, so that, to Lorimer and the other members of the 'Association for the Extension of the Scottish Universities', by the late fifties the prospects for the local academic tradition seemed bleak. In Davie's words, the traditionalists now foresaw 'the ultimate defeat of the intellectual ideals associated with the Scottish way of life'.[17]

Defeat was to take the form, not of total assimilation, but of the compromise which allowed vestiges of the traditional approach to survive alongside a dominant principle which owed nothing to the country's intellectual inheritance. The ideal of a broad and theoretical education, 'general education distinguished by the prominence given to philosophy', as the guiding principle of the university system, was thus laid to rest.

In the twentieth century these arrangements have persisted. At the same time the process of acculturation has continued and deepened, so that today very few are conscious, in any sophisticated way, of an autonomous Scottish intellectual tradition. The nationalism of the seventies, insufficiently sensitive to the cultural dimension, failed to recognise the significance of Davie's contribution, though his work will surely, in the longer term, strengthen cultural resistance (there is already, in the eighties, some evidence of this in the thought of a new generation of intellectuals).

Although the recent period must be seen as one of retreat for Scottish educational ideas, this does not mean that the tradition has shown no signs of vitality. On the contrary, in the twentieth century too, the Scottish educational philosophy was to be re-stated in a powerful form. This re-statement was produced — aptly enough, given the displacement of the native tradition in Scottish universities — not in Scotland but in the University of Sydney, Australia.

III

John Anderson graduated in physics and philosophy from Glasgow in 1917, and was subsequently appointed lecturer in philosophy at Edinburgh, where he remained until his emigration to Sydney in 1926. As Davie has indicated, the mathematics department at Glasgow, the philosophy department at Edinburgh and the Greek department at St Andrews were, during these years, 'focal points in the impassioned, deep debate, then engaging all academic Scotland, as to what was to be the fate, in the modern post-war world, of the highly distinctive system of intellectual values inherited by the country from the Reformation and the Enlightenment — whether this unique legacy of a philosophically centred system of education was to be revitalised to meet the challenges of the times, or allowed to die out finally and forever.' [18]

Anderson would not, in Australia, forget these issues, and as his career progressed, he came to devote more and more attention to them, a concern which culminated in his great essay on classicism of 1959. Anderson was — in Davie's words once more — 'profoundly conscious of the incompatibility between the intellectual values embodied in the traditional Scottish curriculum, and the neo-utilitarian reorganisation of education which in the years after World War II was increasingly undertaken by the various governments of the English-speaking world.'[19] His response was to restate these traditional values against the dominant educational theories of the age.

Anderson does not subscribe, then, to such programmes as 'education for work', 'education for life' or 'education for self-development'; indeed, in such positions Anderson perceived a profoundly *anti-educational* spirit at work. In Eugene Kamenka's phrase, Anderson 'saw no evidence that the theorists of education had educated or educational theories'. [20]

The key to Anderson's educational thought is his opposition to instrumentalist or utilitarian conceptions, the kind of view elicited by such questions as 'what is education for' or 'what is the purpose of education', which imply that education is to be justified in terms of some other, non-educational end. He therefore rejects, for instance, the widely accepted idea that education should foster 'the full development of the personality'. Anderson does not believe, in any case, that this eupeptic notion possesses much coherence (a conviction founded in a Calvinist pessimism about human potentialities); for it depends on the questionable assumption that different talents and faculties can be fully and harmoniously developed. In fact, Anderson argues, 'there are inconsistent possibilities of development, so that when a person develops in one way, that prevents his developing in another way which, to begin with, was equally possible'.[21]

Anderson is concerned above all to combat the pragmatist position he termed 'practicalism'. The practicalist holds that education should be 'for work', 'for life', that it should, in another typical formulation, be 'geared to meet the needs of society', a ghastly phrase which not only smuggles into our thinking a false, consensus view of society, together with related flabby notions like 'the common good' and 'the national interest', but also obliterates the fundamental distinction between *education* and *training*.

In training we acquire practical, useful skills, be they manual, linguistic, mathematical, commercial or whatever. Anderson is not of course concerned to deny that skills are important; what he resists is the confusion, embodied in vocationalist approaches to education, of being trained with being educated.

His own conception of education Anderson characterises as liberal or classical; its distinguishing feature, on the negative side, is that it does not attempt to justify education by reference to some other end, be it the possession of useful skills, the satisfaction of social needs, or the development of a rounded or 'healthy' personality. Positively, the educated life is a life of thought or criticism, understood as 'the examination of all assumptions', or 'the questioning of received opinions and traditions'; education is 'an introduction to culture', which contrasts with 'narrow specialist training', and involves the acquisition of 'a general grasp of the scientific, artistic and social activities of mankind'.

Consistently with these emphases, Anderson was an early critic of the industrialisation and professionalisation of universities. He had no high opinion of the business world ('employers are in general opposed to freedom') and attacked 'the growing invasion of the universities by business interests'. The idea that universities should adapt practices to suit the desires of industry — a view which has become even more popular in recent years — Anderson describes as 'grotesque'.

In a memorable contrast, Anderson writes that education should not be seen as the 'turning out' of teachers, engineers, doctors, but rather as conversion, the turning round of the mind onto its habitual ideas and practices. Education will then also mean critical reflection on one's own life, and its different assumptions, aims and values. Anderson is even ready to accept as an account of education *'the finding of a way of life*, as contrasted with the mere acquisition of arts and accomplishments', [21] a highly significant formulation which serves to deepen the opposition of education, as an inner process of moral-intellectual development, to training, or the learning of skills. An implication of this perspective is that, as the philosopher John Mackie says in an article on Anderson, 'true educational success, the kindling of intellectual interests, the awakening of criticism, cannot be measured by the devices of the psychologist'.[23]

This philosophy of education entailed a number of positions on specific educational issues which were and remain highly controversial, or are now simply totally unfashionable. One is that literature, as 'an embodiment of culture', describing, questioning and evaluating ways of life, is of greater educational significance than science, since it prompts the individual to an examination of his or her own life through a presentation of social and ethical choices, thus contributing to the process of 'finding a way of life'.

> An essentially literary training, as against an essentially scientific training, is to be supported. . .as helping to form a power of judgement, a sense of values. This will be an essential part of the person's subsequent way of life; indeed, it will affect all parts of his life.[24]

Even more offensive to modern, 'enlightened' and 'progressive' opinion is Anderson's defence of classical studies. Anderson is of course aware how anachronistic this position will seem to all 'progressive' schools of thought in education, how absurd it will sound in the centres of intellectual fashion. It is with an acknowledgement of the highly unorthodox nature of his views that Anderson begins the paper — written very late in his career — on classicism, which must surely be regarded as one of the most important and remarkable essays produced by any Scot in the twentieth century.

   To claim educational pre-eminence for the classics, or simply to present classicism as an important view of culture, would commonly in these times be met with ridicule or indifference, since neither the notion of culture nor the classical outlook is now accorded any great respect even in reputedly educated circles. At the outset of the intense struggles, which have occupied the past century or more, over the nature and organisation of education, the conception of it as 'liberal' and hence classical was widespread and apparently well-entrenched. But the position has changed so radically that nowadays it is rare to find any greater concession made to liberal study, either in the narrower sense of concentration on the 'classical tongues' or in the broader sense of attention to the major production of humane letters, than that it is a harmless eccentricity which may still for a time occupy its small corner. What is of special importance, it is widely maintained, is study of the sciences; for, while liberal study had at no time an intrinsically greater capacity for developing the mind, it has under present conditions a very much slighter power of bringing us to a serious grappling with our vital problems. And this is in line with the view which prevails among professional educationists who, even though the main emphasis is not always on science, conceive education as the preparation of the pupil for the problems of the real world in which he is to live, and on that principal dismiss the upholder of tradition as a follower of fantasies.[25]

'Classicism' was published in 1959. In the Britain of the 1980s, it hardly needs saying, practicalism has an even stronger hold on thinking about education than in Anderson's day, and it is now difficult to use the words 'humanist' or 'liberal', with reference to education, without seeming condescending. The utilitarian outlook has achieved such dominance that teachers in the arts subjects, including teachers of classics, often show no awareness of the proper significance of humanist education. Indeed, there is no clearer indication of the victory of practicalist approaches than that the non-scientific subjects too now tend to be defended on the grounds that they serve 'useful' purposes and provide training in skills (English as the teaching of 'language skills', for instance). Teachers of classics can then be reduced to desperate expedients: Latin as a way of training the memory, as a method of studying grammar, or as no more than a way of inculcating 'sustained attention, orderly procedure and perseverance'.[26]

Anderson's slogan is not 'back to Latin', but 'forward to the classics and philosophy'. His arguments for classical studies turn on their potential to encourage the development of critical (or philosophical) intelligence. In the first place, he presents the view that acquaintance with a culture or cultures relatively remote from our own provides knowledge of different ways of thinking, different standards of judgement, an awareness of alternatives, and this involves that distancing from our own practices which is the central dynamic of criticism. Linguistic study has a vital part to play in this process of distancing or alienation: 'the very structure of a foreign language shows us different ways of attacking a subject from those we are accustomed to, those current in our society.'[27] Secondly, the classical languages are particularly appropriate since, for Anderson, they embody 'the classical outlook', which is contrasted with 'prejudice in favour of the local and contemporary', and defined, in 'Classicism', in terms of 'objectivism, criticism, intellectual detachment'. Classical culture is one of the zeniths of the critical, the philosophical spirit, that freedom from narrowness, provincialism and blind adherence to the positive which it is the essence of education to foster. Anderson thinks, indeed, that

> entry into the classical heritage is essential to education in any distinctive sense, that is, the development of criticism or judgement, as contrasted with training in general. [28]

The particular kind of humanist education Anderson supported is hardly likely to find many adherents in the business world or among state functionaries. Anderson knows that no state, and no social group whose main interest is other than the tradition of thought and culture will be happy about institutions which see themselves as centres of critique and dissent rather than servants to 'the national interest', 'the needs of industry', or, for that matter, 'the interests of the working class'. Education in the true sense is a separate interest, and those committed to it, to the practice of criticism and philosophy, must be constantly active in resisting those who wish to subordinate educational institutions to some non-educational end. 'Culture, it cannot be too strongly urged, is a special interest and requires, for its persistence, a certain irreconcilability.'

For Anderson, education is primarily concerned with intellectual development, and his views were attacked, inevitably, for being overly intellectualist. His response to such criticism was that where education was reduced to vocational training or, at another extreme, to the nurturing of the personality and the promotion of psychological security, where, in other words, education as thought was at a discount, the social consequences would be gullibility and acquiescence. Here the 'progressive' view was in the end illiberal, functioning to strengthen existing relations of power.

It is argued that I exaggerate the intellectual element in education, that not all children are fitted for an intellectual training. My answer is that the only alternative to the development of understanding is the development of submissiveness. [29]

All the same, it can readily be admitted that an educational philosophy which makes familiarity with the classical heritage central, insists uncompromisingly on the maintenance of high intellectual standards and conceives the teacher's role as introducing the learner to culture will seem to many *vieux jeu*, an outdated, reactionary, 'elitist' position in a culture where, for some time, concepts such as 'relevance', 'equality' and 'child- centred education' have been prominent in educational debate. If we look beyond the British scene, however — and in particular to France — Anderson's view might begin to seem rather less strange. For in France there is a tradition of strong support, from the left as well as the right, for the maintenance of an intellectual education which restricts itself neither to the interests felt by the child, nor to the demands of economic efficiency or social progress, however conceived; and here the strategy of diluting content and standards for the supposed benefit of working class children is resisted as itself reactionary, since it will merely reinforce their exclusion from the world of learning and higher culture. The Italian left has tended to similar positions, partly due to the influence of Gramsci, whose ideas on education, with their emphasis on struggle and rigour, would be unpalatable to most of those members of the British left who have been involved in the recent Gramsci cult.[30]

We recall that Anderson was not impressed by the orthodox educationists of the day. If he could survey the present education scene in Scotland, he would, to put the matter charitably, find little to make him reconsider his judgment. The prevailing discourse is practicalist-behaviourist, characterised by expressions like 'practical skills', 'social skills', 'preparation for life', and the rest, a lexis which bespeaks collapse to those approaches Anderson identifies as inimical to what is genuinely educational.

This intellectual poverty is the prerogative neither of the right nor the left; but since the Labour Party at present enjoys an overwhelming political ascendancy in Scotland, let us mention by way of illustration the programme devoted to education in the major BBC 1 Scotland series, 'Scotland 2000', broadcast in 1987, where a labourist, 'radical' analysis of Scottish education was presented. [31] Education, the programme asserted, should have personal, social and vocational goals: the pupil should emerge from school self-confident, good at getting on with others and possessed of relevant vocational skills. Now these are, no doubt, desirable qualities — but they have nothing to do with being educated.

The film was also a typical product of 'progressive' thinking in its argument that education should be 'fun', always 'interesting' and enjoyable — as if challenge, sacrifice, complexity, difficulty, struggle were not, too, intrinsic to any worthwhile human project, including the attempt to enter into the educated life.

Where education is taken to be the promotion of psychological well-being and the teaching of vocational skills; where 'interest' and 'enjoyment' become overriding criteria (as if the teacher were in competition with the purveyors of television and other junk culture); where the notion that education is exacting and arduous loses purchase — there we are surely in the situation Anderson warned of, where the main function of schools is to condemn the populace to philistinism.

Despite the work of educational 'theorists' and 'experts', there will be many teachers who continue to honour humanist ideals and the educational values Anderson articulated. What is now required on the part of those committed to our educational traditions, is greater intransigence against the anti-educational forces operating within and outside educational institutions, on the left as well as the right. This will mean, for instance, fighting for the survival of classics, and the extension of modern foreign language teaching. It will mean asserting, against those who stress what children will 'need' in later life, the importance of the study of history, as a confrontation with ways of thought and action different from our own, and as an engagement with the traditions the child inherits, and from which he or she will be able to fashion their own way of life. It will mean being critical of tendencies in English teaching to emphasise the learning of skills at the expense of the study of literature.[32]

But we should also be considering more adventurous measures. The most important step towards the re-assertion of the Scottish intellectual tradition in our educational system would be the re-instatement of philosophy as a central study. This could be achieved by the establishment at the later secondary stage of a *'classe de philosophie'* which would serve to introduce pupils to the world of theory and ideas. Such an arrangement would reflect the aspirations of a man Anderson greatly admired, the St Andrews philosopher and classicist John Burnet, who, after World War One, urged the restructuring of education along traditional lines, with philosophy restored to a dominant position, in the belief that too much had been conceded in Scotland to specializing and pragmatist tendencies which were incompatible with local cultural traditions.

In all this, Anderson is a powerful ally, providing the rigorous, worked-out position which those who attempt to defend humanist education seem mostly to lack. We desperately need his eloquent insistence that education is not training or a form of psychotherapy; that there are higher goals than the acquisition of useful skills; that 'the finding of a way of life', and not preparation for everyday life, is the essence of education.

The interest and importance of Anderson's theory of education can hardly be exaggerated. To quote Kamenka:

> Anderson said the important and central things without which we can have no philosophy of education. . . no conception of either education or culture as central and complex human traditions. . . [33]

7

Scottish Thought
in the Twentieth Century

It is a central tenet of the Scottish intelligentsia's received wisdom concerning the history of their culture that, after the achievements of figures like Hume and Smith in the eighteenth century, Scots ceased to contribute in any significant fashion to the world of philosophy and ideas. On this view, Scotland has since been an intellectual wasteland. A full response to this position is beyond the scope of this volume ; but, ignoring entirely the fascinating, as yet almost wholly unexplored intellectual culture of nineteenth-century Scotland, and its major figures (Hamilton, Ferrier, Robertson Smith, Frazer, Flint, Seth et al), as well as a good number of more recent thinkers, we will now sketch the outline of a refutation of the received view, focusing in particular on the work of John Anderson, John Macmurray, R.D. Laing and Alasdair MacIntyre.

But mention should be made too, in passing, of the tradition of philosophical and theological scholarship in twentieth-century Scotland, the major landmarks here including the work of John Burnet on Greek philosophy, of Norman Kemp Smith on Hume, and of Kemp Smith, H. J. Paton and others on Kant, making Scotland — in the words of Lewis White Beck in a recent issue of *Kant Studien* — over the last hundred years a 'world-centre' of Kant scholarship.

For most readers, the divinity departments of the Scottish universities will seem an unlikely source of ideas and intellectual excitement. But this is another prejudice about Scottish intellectual life which does not survive closer examination. For in fact Scottish theologians, displaying a very unEnglish Germanophilia, have made a significant contribution to the intellectual culture of the English-speaking world by translating and interpreting the work of such figures as Martin Buber, Dietrich Bonhoeffer, Karl Barth, Rudolf Bultmann and Martin Heidegger, outstanding examples being the contributions of Ronald Gregor Smith, Ian Henderson, Thomas Torrance and John Macquarrie.[1]

I

John Anderson was born in Stonehouse, Lanarkshire in 1893, the son of a radical headmaster, and went on to study physics and philosophy at Glasgow. Colleague for a time of Kemp Smith in the philosophy department at Edinburgh, he left Scotland in 1926 for Australia to take up a philosophy chair at Sydney. There he established himself as both a major intellectual force and a somewhat notorious public figure, on account of his unconventional views and a certain relish for polemic.

If Anderson has only recently begun to receive any public attention in Scotland[2], he has long enjoyed a remarkable reputation in Australia, where he taught and influenced the likes of Passmore, Kamenka, Armstrong and Mackie. In the eyes of theoretically-minded students, he occupied a unique and dominant position on the intellectual scene: a kind of *maitre à penser*, a radical, unconventional theorist, suspicious of academic and political orthodoxies, who offered sharp and powerful criticism of received ideas in philosophy, politics, social theory and education. Something of the esteem in which Anderson has been held is communicated in the comments of his student, the philospher and historian of ideas Eugene Kamenka:

> John Anderson, in his long career as Challis Professor of Philosophy in the University of Sydney, displayed a combination of unflagging logical incisiveness and acuteness, an outstanding sense of coherence and connection, and an unusually strong and original capacity for creative theoretical imagination.[3]

Anderson impressed by the rigour of his thinking; by his insistence that the philosopher should be active in social and political life, addressing the great issues of the day; and by his commitment to the view that philosophical inquiry is the heart of culture.

He impressed despite, or perhaps because of the fact that his ideas were seldom compatible with those in fashion. Wittgenstein once observed that 'a philosopher is not a member of any intellectual community [*kein Burger einer Denkgemeinde*]; and it is just this which makes him a philosopher.' A better illustration of the remark than Anderson's life and work could hardly be found. Far from acquiescing in the cultural trends and intellectual orthodoxies of the day, Anderson made it his concern to attack them, exposing the shallowness and confusions of the ideas propagated by journalists, politicians and experts, the 'reputedly educated'. He was, comments

Armstrong, not an iconoclast, but a 'meta-iconoclast'; and his thinking was devoid of any tendermindedness. [4] Kamenka suggests that this view of the philosopher as a critic and dissident was rooted in his background, in 'a certain Presbyterian intransigence, a Scottish suspicion of things English, of urbanity and self-satisfaction. . .'

In *The Crisis of the Democratic Intellect*, George Davie presents the thesis that the distinctive Scottish contribution to twentieth-century philosophy lies in a critique of modernist optimism which can be read as a secular reassertion of Calvinist notions about human fallibility. This is expressed, for instance, in the anti-evolutionist epistemology of Norman Kemp Smith, who held that knowledge does not develop in a cumulative fashion, but rather, in Davie's words, 'in the course of a critical struggle against illusions which at every turn reassert themselves in new forms after they have been conquered.'[5] But this strain of modern Scottish thought finds its most eloquent and complex articulation, Davie suggests, in the work of Anderson. 'Anti-modernism' is certainly a useful description of the position Anderson developed. This anti-modernism is crystallised in his philosophy of education, where he opposes the dominant 'progressive' theories of the age. He criticised both the idea of education as self-expression or self-discovery, and the vocationalist approach he named 'practicalism', according to which education should be organised on utilitarian lines, with pride of place given to the practical, technical and scientific subjects. Such philosophies confuse education with quite different things — in the case of practicalism, with training or the acquisition of skills. Anderson, for his part, talks of education in terms of thought, criticism, the awakening of intellectual interests, an introduction to culture, 'the questioning of received opinions', 'the finding of a way of life'. Essential to the development of critical intelligence, he argued, was cultural comparison, acquaintance with a variety of judgements (a view which helps us to understand his defence of classics). Unfashionably, again, he took literature to be of greater educational significance than science, since it aids the pupil to work out the 'way of life' he or she will adopt. Attacked, inevitably, as an elitist, Anderson replied that only an education which stressed ideas and the extension of powers of critical thought could, in the end, be a radical social force.

In his later philosophy Anderson expressed a deep distrust of all progressive, reformist and meliorist discourse, attacking the cheap optimism of those who envisaged a New Jerusalem organised by the planners and experts on the basis of the judicious application of science and technology. Progressivists, he argued, overlook 'qualitative distinctions and oppositions', neglect the incompatibility of different values and traditions, different moralities and forms of life, and collapse ethics to questions of distribution.

Anderson's break with his early Marxism, his view of the role of traditions in forming individuals and determining their potentialities, his opposition to progressivism, meliorism or 'the reforming attitude', his insistence that education and culture are separate interests which do not serve some other ends — all this might suggest that, like so many disillusioned intellectuals of the time, Anderson ended up in the conservative camp. In fact, his political thought fitted no orthodoxy, and his position is too complex to be adjusted to any crude 'left-right' dichotomy. It retained a Marxist streak, as when he attacked welfarism as a form of 'bourgeois philanthropy', functioning 'to sidetrack on the one hand, and on the other hand to justify the repression of, those independent movements which would alter the balance of social power.'

Anderson's Marxism developed, partly under the influence of Sorel, into a position of great subtlety and insight. He criticised the tendency of leftist thought to concentrate on questions of property rather than control (an issue recently explored by Foucault). He argued that the working class was losing direction through its acceptance of consumer values (in this respect he shared something of the position of the Frankfurt School). He was an early, trenchant critic of the welfarism and statism which were coming to dominate the thinking of the labour movement. State provision is incompatible with freedom and equality, which cannot be granted but have to be achieved: it is 'not by what they are given, that men will win release from their servitude'; 'genuine equality depends on people's own efforts and is not something that can be bestowed'. It is also foolish to rely on a 'protective' state for the provision of benefits since states will function, ultimately, only for the benefit of those who work for them. But the deepest objection to labourism was that, by pandering to the desire for protection and security, it was fostering a servile mentality. Labourism was in fact the enemy of enterprise, liberty and responsibility.[6]

II

The main focus of many recent Scottish contributions to theory is the development of a culture in which science has achieved intellectual preeminence. Specifically, here we frequently encounter challenges to the claim (embedded in the culture of analytic philosophy) that scientific reasoning represents the primary mode of human cognition; and at the same time anxiety about the ethical and personal consequences of the triumph of the 'scientific worldview'.

One central argument of these contributions is that empiricism or 'the naturalistic viewpoint' involves an arbitrary and illegitimate restriction of the concepts of experience, knowledge and reality. This has, for instance, been a major theme in the work of John Macquarrie (co-translator of the the English edition of Heidegger's *Sein und Zeit*, and the author of popular accounts of existentialism). Macquarrie presents one of his recent books, *In Search of Humanity*, as a 'plea for a wider concept of knowing' than that which is inscribed in the Cartesian epistemological tradition. Knowledge of natural fact is only one mode of cognition. We ought also, he urges, to take seriously such modalities of knowledge as conscience, which should not be seen as an agency of censure and rebuke, but an inner voice which reveals the gap between the empirical and the actual self, and indicates what we ought to be or become. Our understanding of knowledge has been restricted, too, by the belief that knowledge demands detachment from its object. Certain forms of knowledge require a coming together of the knower and the known. 'In many subjects, and not least in the study of humanity itself, the idea of detachment is a hindrance.' Knowing another involves an attempt at union with and participation in the world of the other. Macquarrie comments on the concept of knowledge implied in the text 'Now Adam knew his wife Eve. . .' that 'it is an indication of the extent to which we have fallen away from that understanding of knowing by union and participation that modern translations of the Bible substitute quite different ideas, and fail entirely either to comprehend or express what was meant by 'knowing'.[7] Macquarrie's aim is to establish 'a more human concept of knowledge'. This does not mean 'more subjective', 'but rather the opposite, for the broader concept of knowledge being advocated rests on a correspondingly broader apprehension of the reality with which we are confronted.'

That we should attend to all the different dimensions of human experience — and in particular our consciousness of a moral order — is a main theme too in the work of John Baillie. 'I must trust my experience,' he wrote, 'my sense experience, my social experience and my moral experience.' Baillie was anxious to contest the notion, propagated by the positivists, that truth and certainty can be predicted only of natural scientific propositions: 'There is nothing of which I am more assured than that I must not exploit my fellow man in the interest of my own selfish gain, but must seek his own good no less than my own and, if need be, at the cost of my own. There is nothing of which I am more assured than that Hitler was wrong in attempting to exterminate the Jews.'[8]

But Baillie goes further than claiming that our ideas of experience, knowledge and reality should not be limited in their application only to the natural world by arguing that it is our knowledge of persons, rather than knowledge of natural fact, which is primary and paradigmatic, and that it is in our dealings with others that we are most assuredly in contact with reality. 'To my mind knowledge of persons is the very type and pattern of what we mean by knowledge. Of no other existents is our knowledge so intimate and direct.'

'Reality is personal', Baillie had written in an earlier work. He supports this way of seeing the world in different ways. Reality can be conceived as that which resists. 'Reality is what I "come up against", what takes me by surprise, the other-than-myself which pulls me up and obliges me to reckon with it and adjust myself to it because it will not consent simply to adjust itself to me. . .The world of natural objects, real as it is on its own level, offers to my will a much less stubborn resistance than that offered by my encounter with my fellow men.'

We can also think of reality as that which is present to us. It is then significant that 'we do not normally speak of the presence of a physical object'. Nor do we talk of 'being with' an object. 'It is only persons that I can be with. (Baillie acknowledges his debt here to a number of existentialist and personalist thinkers: Heidegger, Eberhard Grisebach, Gabriel Marcel and, above all, Martin Buber, the German-Jewish philosopher whose teaching that 'others are the real world' has found such resonance among Scottish thinkers.)

It follows from Baillie's view that it is the interpersonal world we inhabit which should be our main theoretical and practical concern. He feared, however, that the spread of scientism, with its identification of reality with the realm of natural fact, was undermining our social and moral senses.

Both Baillie and Macquarrie acknowledge the influence of John Macmurray, who should be seen as the leading figure of a Scottish school which, through a critique of scientism, develops a 'personalist' approach to the world. Macmurray is now a neglected writer (none of his books is currently in print), but he may yet come to be recognised as one of the most interesting and fertile of recent Scottish theorists.

The important philosophical issues, Macmurray held, are not dictated by academic tradition: they are pressed upon the philosopher by the circumstances of the times. So his own philosophy is a response to what he sees as the central issue of his age, a cultural predicament he terms 'a crisis of the personal'. Critical of the analytic movement in which he saw a failure to engage with the vital questions, he had some sympathy with the existentialists, whose 'sensitiveness to the darkness of human despair leads them to discover the emergent problem of our time,' as he wrote in *The Self as Agent.*

The weakening of religious forms of life, Macmurray argues, is both a symptom and an agency of the impoverishment of our lives as persons, for religious consciousness has served to inculcate the practice of self-criticism, to foster the interior life, and to uphold the categories of personal responsibility and personal merit. The waning of religion therefore signals a profound and alarming cultural development, involving increasing 'loss of the human subject', to borrow a phrase from Ronald Gregor Smith. In emphasising the importance of religious traditions for the maintenance of ways of living which attempt to do justice to our nature as persons, Macmurray is at eloquent variance with the facile secularism of most contemporary thought.

> The decline of religious influence and of religious practice . . . betrays, and in turn intensifies, a growing insensitiveness to the personal aspects of life, and a growing indifference to personal values. Christianity, in particular, is the exponent and the guardian of the personal, and the function of organised Christianity in our history has been to foster and maintain the personal life and to bear continuous witness, in symbol and doctrine, to the ultimacy of personal values. If this influence is removed or ceases to be effective, the awareness of personal issues will tend to be lost, in the pressure of functional preoccupations, by all except those who are by nature specially sensitive to them. The sense of personal dignity as well as of personal unworthiness will tend to atrophy, with the decline in habits of self examination. Success will tend to become the criterion of rightness, and there will spread through society a temper which is extraverted, pragmatic and merely objective, for which all problems are soluble by better organisation.[9]

Macmurray's project can be conceived as a foregrounding of the phenomenon of personal being in face of the 'crisis of the personal'. This crisis has a theoretical dimension. We have been led astray, Macmurray believes, by a set of beliefs concerning reason, knowledge, the intellect, the emotions and the self. In what amounts to a quite remarkable contribution to theory, he proceeds to offer what we should nowadays perhaps call a deconstruction of the whole way of approaching the world and our experience of it which the successes of natural science has rendered dominant. (If critiques of scientism are today no longer new, we should bear in mind that Macmurray was developing and publishing those ideas from the early 1930s.)

Again, there is no question of any espousal of irrationalism. 'Our real nature as persons is to be reasonable and to extend our capacity for reason.' But Macmurray rejects the customary and enduring identification of reason with thought or intellect. The equation of reason with 'passionless reflection', and the divorce of reason and emotion are, he argues, 'quite arbitrary and groundless'. Detached, unfeeling reflection is rational, 'but it has no unique claim to rationality, and it is indeed not the primary expression of reason.' He suggests that reason be understood in terms of objectivity rather than intellection: 'reason is the capacity to behave in terms of the nature of the object.' And emotions, like thoughts, can be objective — i.e. appropriate to the reality to which they refer. At the same time, Macmurray sees no grounds for distinguishing feelings and thoughts in terms of the 'subjective' nature of the former, since the latter are also, in the same sense, subjective.

> If our feelings are subjective because they occur in us, why not our thoughts which as surely occur to us? If our thoughts are objective because they refer to objects, then our feelings, which refer to objects in their own fashion, are objective also.

It is, then, a mistake to disesteem our valuations and feelings about the world, to dismiss them, simply because they are feelings, as 'irrational' and 'merely subjective'.

Like Baillie and Macquarrie, Macmurray is opposed to the positivist identification of knowledge with natural scientific knowledge. He reverses the conventional notion that art is somehow less objective than science, less concerned with things as they really are, by arguing that science, which is concerned with general properties rather than individual things, yields a more superficial form of knowledge: scientific knowledge is knowledge *about* things, not knowledge *of* them. If we have to choose, we must say that it is the person with the artist's sensibility rather than the scientist's, who really knows the world.

Our thinking about the nature of the self is also in need of revision. The self is customarily conceived, in the Cartesian tradition, as an observer and as an individual. As against this, Macmurray wishes to see the self as an agent and a person. We ought, he thinks, to abandon the quest for pure and certain knowledge (which in any case is illusory) in order to assess our thinking in terms of its contribution to the extension of community and friendship. All thinking, he wrote, is for the sake of action, and all action for the sake of friendship. The second important idea here is that the self is not an individual but a person, and persons are constituted by their relations with other persons.

We can perhaps best understand Macmurray's critique of contemporary culture as a warning — a warning of a world composed of selves concerned with the 'merely objective' and focused only on outward success, cut off from others in an individualist way of thinking which results in a diminished subjectivity, insensitive to the obligations involved in the leading of a rich, fully human life.

It is important to emphasise that these personalist theorists are not proposing some form of withdrawn inwardness: personal life, they argue, has an inextricable personal or communal dimension. Macquarrie wishes us to see our lives as the 'task of becoming a person', but, he adds, 'it might be more accurate to say that the goal is to become a person-in-community, for no person exists in isolation, though a self may try to do so, and in so doing diminish its own personhood.' For Ronald Gregor Smith, the Glasgow theologian and Buber translator, 'it is as persons along with other persons that true humanity consists. True humanity is community.'[11]

The existence of what we have here termed the Scottish personalist school (Macmurray, Baillie, Gregor Smith, Macquarrie) has so far escaped the attention of historians of twentieth-century Scotland. However, preoccupations of the school were to surface in the 1960s, in the work of one of the few recent Scottish thinkers who has reached a wide audience and made an impact on public debate: the psychiatrist R.D.Laing. But before we consider Laing's contribution, let us turn to the ideas of another Glaswegian, Alasdair MacIntyre.

III

MacIntyre, born in 1929, is one of the leading moral theorists of the age. His *After Virtue* (1981 and 1985) has generated an extraordinary level of interest, in many different countries, among philosophers, theologians and a non-specialist reading public, permitting MacIntyre to say, with reference to the position developed in that book, that

> I have some assurance that what I articulated was not just something thought by me, but something thought and felt by large numbers of people who recognize themselves as unable to be heard saying what they really mean in modern societies.[12]

After Virtue is a critique of contemporary views of ethics and contemporary social forms, and at the same time nothing less than an attempt, based on an analysis of the historical development of Western ethical theory, to restructure the way we think about morality, the way we conceive the human self, and the way in which we live our lives. Clearly, this is an awesome project, remarkable for its originality, its seriousness, and its sheer intellectual scope: the *dramatis personae* of *After Virtue*'s intricate plot include among many others Sophocles, Aristotle, Aquinas, Hume, Diderot, Kant, Kierkegaard, Nietzsche, Marx, Mill, Austen, Weber, Sartre and Rawls. It would be hard to identify, certainly in the English-speaking world, any current intellectual venture of similar ambition, depth and import.

After Virtue begins with the contention that, notwithstanding the appeal to moral considerations made in many contemporary disputes, we now live in a culture where the moral life is under severe threat because our understanding of ethics has been almost wholly eroded. Fragments of ethical discourse survive, but there is now no available ethical system which could invest our views with coherence and intelligibility. 'We possess indeed simulacra of morality. . . But we have — very largely, if not entirely — lost our comprehension, both theoretical and practical, of morality'.[13] This is a situation out of which no purely descriptive philosophy, be it analytical or phenomenological, can lead us, for descriptive philosophies can only recount our fragmented moral discourse and moral experience.

MacIntyre's view that we have no proper conception of ethics can of course only be understood within the totality of his argument. But this particular starting-point — a philosophically informed sense of a grave crisis in ethics — is itself worthy of comment, for it links MacIntyre with a number of other recent Scottish thinkers for whom also the key issue of our time is the threat posed to the moral life. Like them, MacIntyre locates the main source of this threat in certain modern modes of thought, and specifically in currents which present moral beliefs as based on individual choices and preferences.

This cultural placing is intended also as a corrective to the reading presented in Inglis' *Radical Earnestness*, according to which MacIntyre is representative of an alternative English intellectual tradition.[14] There is, simply, no theoretical affinity between English new leftism (Thompson, Hill, Hobsbawm et al) and the MacIntyre of *After Virtue*, an obvious point which only the deployment of a catch-all concept like 'radical earnestness' could obscure. MacIntyre explicitly distinguishes his own position that our moral discourse is deeply incoherent from that of the modern radical, who takes our existing moral resources for granted. (See also the comments below on MacIntyre's attitude to Marxism.)

To follow MacIntyre's terminology, the dominant moral theory in contemporary thought is emotivism; and it is emotivism which informs everyday attitudes to morality throughout our culture:

> people now think, talk and act as if emotivism were true. . .Emotivism has become embodied in our culture.[15]

An emotivist view of ethics is, we might say, now part of our *Lebenswelt*, the store of unarticulated theory which lies behind everyday action and opinion.

In histories of philosophy emotivism is described as the metaethical theory — principally associated with C.L. Stevenson — that statements about duty, goodness and so on express the speaker's feelings and attitudes, and aim at persuading others to adopt these same attitudes. So 'this is good' means 'I approve of this; please do so too'. The formidable semantic difficulties involved in this account of the meaning of moral assertions need not detain us here. What is crucial for the argument is that in emotivism morality is conceived as a question of individual choice and taste, the possibility of objective ethical criteria is denied, and a strict division is established between the realm of fact and truth, and the realm of value.

MacIntyre uses the term 'emotivism' to refer to the general subjectivist position according to which moral views do not permit of rational warrant. Thus Sartrean existentialism, with its stress on individual choice, is also emotivist; and MacIntyre presents Weber as another architect of the emotivist worldview, since in Weber reason is primarily instrumental, *Zweckrationalität*, concerned with calculating means to the achievement of ends which can only be determined by an irrefutable personal *Entscheidung*. The latest sophisticated exponents of liberal theory (such as Dworkin) also subscribe to the basic premise ef emotivism in conceiving questions about the nature of the good life as unsettlable in principle. The enemy includes liberalism.

Readers for whom the crucial present intellectual conflict is between Marxist and non-Marxist forms of thought may at this stage be experiencing a certain disquiet: where does Marxism fit into the picture? MacIntyre draws attention to a contradiction in Marxist theory which reveals a serious inadequacy. On the one hand Marxists complain, no doubt correctly, that the capitalist order is morally bankrupt. At the same time they are committed to the view that advanced bourgeois society contains all the prerequisites of a truly human, socialist society. But if the first assessment is correct, the second is highly implausible. If, in other words, capitalist society is composed of individuals who are acquisitive, self-seeking and morally deficient in other respects, where are the human resources for the creation of the good society? 'It is not surprising,' comments MacIntyre, 'that at this point Marxism tends to produce its own versions of the *Übermensch*: Lukacs's ideal proletarian, Leninism's ideal revolutionary'.[16] The response to the Marxist, then, on the relevance of MacIntyre's concern with moral disorder is that such a project is itself necessitated by a fundamental Marxist premise (the ethical impoverishment of capitalist culture) — unless Marxists are content with flights of fantasy.

A, or perhaps the, major symptom of the moral bankruptcy of the present cultural order is the intellectual dominance of emotivism, with its consignment of moral positions to a realm of choice, decision and feeling beyond the operations of reason and the purchase of concepts like truth and error. MacIntyre's work is informed by a sense of the wider import of what at first sight might seem to be abstract and remote theoretical issues. 'Philosophical ideas', he writes in *Marcuse*, 'are influential in social, moral and political life'.[17] Ineluctably, on this premise, the triumph of decisionism in its various forms will have wide-reaching effects on the texture of everyday life in our society. One such effect is the prevalence of protest as a vehicle for the articulation of moral beliefs and the assertion of moral rights, protest being a mode which expresses lack of conviction in the possibility of reasoned argument. The relegation of the ethical can be seen, too, more significantly, in the kinds of figure who function in our society as cultural exemplars; the rich connoisseur, dedicated to the maximisation of individual satisfaction, and to this end a 'consumer of persons'; the manager, whose prized skill is the putative ability to manipulate others; therapists, analysts, *et hoc genus omne*, not typically concerned with questions of goodness or the pursuit of virtue, but with finding the best means to the achievement of ends such as 'adjustment'

It is a major — and, in modern Anglo-American philosophy, unusual — feature of *After Virtue* that it places questions about the nature of the human self at the heart of moral theory, and challenges us to confront the conception of ourselves inscribed in the way we live.

MacIntyre is then concerned to make explicit the remarkable view of the self which is embedded in emotivism. The singularity of the modern self is best understood in contrast with the pre-modern or classical conception, which contains two features its later counterpart has lost. The first is what we might call a social or inter-personal component. In the classical tradition, I am what I am, I am myself, partially in virtue of my occupation of a position in a particular social and historical nexus, as the child of this parent, the parent of this child, as a member of this village, community, tribe. On this view,

> These are not characteristics that belong to human beings accidentally, to be stripped away in order to discover 'the real me'. They are part of my substance. . .[18]

Secondly, the classical self is conceived as being, at any given time, at a point on a journey, moving, or failing to move, towards a certain destination, pursuing a trajectory which forms the object of ethical evaluation.

The modern self, *per contra*, is a stripped-down, desocialised, dehistoricised self: we might say, if we accept Macmurray's account that persons are constituted by relations with other persons, that it is a depersonalised self. For, in emotivist theories of ethics, the essence of moral agency resides precisely in the self's ability to stand back from each and every contingency in order to choose freely the composition of its moral world. To take, by way of illustration, two of MacIntyre's own examples, the view that 'the self is detachable from its social and historical roles and statuses' is displayed by young Germans of today who believe that the 1933-45 period is not morally relevant to their relationships with Jewish contemporaries, and by English people who deny all personal implication in the present-day conflicts in Ireland.[19]

At the same time, MacIntyre claims, the practice of judging from an ethical standpoint the trajectory charted by a whole human life has been lost.

> The conception of a whole human life as the primary subject of objective and impersonal evaluation, of a type of evaluation which provides the content for judgement upon the particular actions or projects of a given individual, is something that ceases to be generally available at some point in the progress—if we can call it such—towards and into modernity.[20]

To summarise, then, 'the peculiarly modern , the emotivist self, in acquiring sovereignty in its own realm lost its traditional boundaries provided by a social identity and a view of human life as ordered to a given end'.[21]

Once more, a particular philosophy will correlate with a particular social formation, and MacIntyre's remarkable analysis of modern self-comprehension can generate a rich *Kulturkritik* which he has time only now and then to hint at. Deprived of the conception of life as a narrative unity, the modern individual is preoccupied with the present moment. The aesthetic mode achieves dominance, and variety, as Kierkegaard puts it, becomes 'the highest law of life'.

MacIntyre proceeds to trace, back through the utilitarians, Kierkegaard, Kant and Hume, the complex history of the process which issues in the emotivist world we now all inhabit. But this is not, in the manner of 'normal' history, a value-free chronicle of shifting intellectual trends. MacIntyre's history is 'informed by standards', and his evaluation is that all modern ethical systems have been doomed to failure, unable to present the intelligibility of the moral life. For, he argues, with the rupture from the Aristotelian tradition signalled by Cartesianism and Protestantism, an essential component of any viable ethical scheme was lost.

The classical or Aristotelian system (as set out in the *Nicomachean Ethics*) has three basic elements: first, a description of what MacIntyre terms 'untutored human-nature-as-it-happens-to-be'; second, a view of 'human-nature-as-it-would-be-if-it-realised-its-telos'; and third, ethics as the form of knowledge which helps us to pass from the untutored to the ethical self. When Aristotelian science was rejected, the teleological view of man — 'man as having an essence which defines his true end' — was rejected too. But with the disappearance of the second element in the classical moral scheme — a conception of the proper end of a human life — we are left with two unconnected and unconnectable strands.

> Since the whole point of ethics. . . is to enable man to pass from his present state to his true end, the elimination of any notion of essential human nature and with it the abandonment of any notion of a telos leaves behind a moral scheme composed of two remaining elements whose relationship becomes quite unclear.

As Hume was famously to assert, there is now no possibility of any passage from an 'is' (unreconstructed human nature) to any 'ought' (the various maxims and injunctions of our moral discourse). Where morality is divorced from the conception of an *ultimus finis* of human life, it begins to appear incomprehensible, beyond rational redemption. Or, to put the matter more prosaically, there is now no longer any reason for not simply pursuing the self-interest of the pre-ethical self, and not indulging in a bit of immorality if you can get away with it.

MacIntyre is concerned to question not only emotivism and liberalism, but the whole intellectual tradition of which they are the outcome. It is modernity itself which is being challenged. And against modernity, MacIntyre intends to re-assert the classical-Aristotelian conception of ethics and the self.

MacIntyre's reconstruction of Aristotelianism places the virtues at the heart of ethics and presents the virtuous life as the only one in and through which the proper end of human life, eudaimonia or 'well-being', can be achieved — which does not mean, of course, that the wicked may not prosper, or that the attempt to lead a good life is always compatible with the attainment of 'external' goods such as wealth, fame and power. The virtues are learned and exercised in striving for the goods internal to human practices— in striving to be good teachers, good parents, good footballers and, beyond this, in the life which does not lose sight of the necessity to continue asking what it is that constitutes the good life, the life which continually poses the question: 'what sort of person am I to become?' [22]

It would be superfluous to stress how radically MacIntyre's moral theory departs from dominant contemporary values and discursive modes. His achievement is to have demonstrated, against these barbaric forces, in 'the new dark ages which are already upon us', the intelligibility of the ethical, to have opened up a space in which it may be possible to understand the nature and significance of a good, a human life. We could hardly, of any thinker, ask for more.

IV

R.D.Laing's first book, *The Divided Self*, was published in 1960, shortly before the appearance of Michel Foucault's *Folie et Deraison* (1961). Together with Foucault's study, Laing's critique of conventional psychiatry was instrumental in initiating an important debate about psychiatric practice, its conceptual apparatus and socio-political functions. Laing became one of the *lumières* of new leftism, and the only Scot to gain entry to the Fontana Modern Masters pantheon.

But if Laing has been widely recognised as an important figure, to date there has been no attempt to explore with any seriousness the cultural background of his thought. Most available studies — such as Friedenberg's volume in the Modern Masters series, and the *Laing and Anti-Psychiatry* collection edited by Boyers and Orrill — make next to no mention of the Scottish background, and fail entirely to examine the possibility that Laing's ideas might be locatable within Scottish intellectual traditions. The reason for this, of course, is the assumption we referred to above — that modern Scotland is a cultural wasteland. To put the view simply: Laing cannot be inserted into a Scottish tradition, because there are here no vital intellectual traditions.

Of course, there is a common journalistic way of placing Laing which does emphasise his Scottish origins (this has been popular with *Guardian* and *Times Literary Supplement* reviewers). On this account Laing upholds a Scottish tradition of interest in divided or schizoid personalities, a concern which is taken to reflect the pervasiveness of a distinctively profound schism in both the Scottish psyche and Scottish society. Within this reading, Scottish culture is defined in an entirely negative way, identified as something freakish and pathological.

Such interpretations, which conveniently require no close knowledge of Scottish intellectual traditions, seem often, in fact, to be motivated by crude anti-Scottish prejudice. This is apparent in the following extract from a *Guardian* feature on Laing. Commenting on what he sees as Laing's shifting allegiances, the author writes:

> Clearly Dr Laing is himself somewhat divided, as are so many Scotsmen. Highlands and Lowlands, cold rationalists and Calvinist fanatics, Glasgow and Edinburgh, teetotallers and dram-drinkers. Perhaps *Divided Self* should be seen in a tradition that includes such other works by Scots as Stevenson's *Dr Jekyll and Mr Hyde* and Hogg's *Confessions of a Justified Sinner*.[23]

Predictably, our own reviewers have not been slow to adopt this inferiorist perspective. Alan Bold, for instance, presents Laing's work as an investigation of the 'internal division' which, he would have us believe, is definitive of the Scottish world.[24] The aim here is to take a broader view of Laing's work (looking beyond *The Divided Self*), and to relate this achievement to a specific cultural milieu. The significance of Laing's Glasgow University education has recently been indicated by George Davie, who draws attention to the 'German-Hegelian' orientation of the Glasgow philosophy department, a tradition which survived down to the sixties, and the phenomenological concerns of certain of its members (most notably J.J.Russell). When the department succumbed to the Oxbridge analytic regime, Davie argues, the Glasgow philosophical tradition survived in the work of psychiatrists such as Laing:

> The departure of Russell did not mean the extinction of the phenomenological interests within the Glasgow Arts area of studies. Suppressed within the Philosophy Department, Russell's project of using phenomenology to reanimate the intellectual life of Britain reappeared among Glasgow psychiatrists, and was realised in practice with striking success by Ronald Laing. . .[25]

This goes some way towards dispelling ignorance about the intellectual roots of Laing's work — the range of reading in Contintental thought displayed in *The Divided Self*, for instance, and that work's phenomenological discourse. But to understand the specific inflections given by Laing to the existentialist-phenomenological approach, it is necessary to explore the work's filiations with the ideas of the Scottish personalists we have discussed above. This allows, we believe, the development of a new perspective on Laing's achievement.

A foregrounding of the phenomenon of personhood; an insistence that knowledge is not exhausted in scientific cognition; hostility to the disestimation of important aspects of human experience which the triumphs of science have encouraged — those parameters of the ideas of the Scottish personalist school largely define the nature of Laing's intellectual career also.

In *The Divided Self*, Laing's critique of conventional psychiatry centres on the failure (itself, he suggests, an instance of madness) to approach the patient as a person. 'We shall be concerned', he writes, 'with people who experience themselves as automata, as robots, as bits of machinery, or even as animals. Such persons are rightly regarded as crazy. Yet why do we not regard a theory which seeks to transmute persons into automata or animals as equally crazy?'[26] The depersonalisation of the human being in established psychiatric theory means that the task of constructing an authentic study of persons has hardly yet begun.

Macmurray had insisted that the self cannot be understood as a substance or an organism, but only as a person. Laing quotes him to this effect in the opening chapter of *The Divided Self*; Macmurray is in fact the only thinker whose ideas are discussed there.

Behind attempts to account for human behaviour in chemical, mechanical and biological terms, Laing argues, lurks the belief that only via such approaches can scientificity be attained. 'There is a common illusion that one can somehow increase one's understanding of a person if one can translate a personal understanding of him into the impersonal terms of a sequence of it-processes.' However, the 'objectivity' thus attained is pseudo-scientific. Laing proposes an approach which, in contrast, emphasises on the one hand the person's desires, hopes, fears, intentions, projects, his/her own conception of their being, and on the other the social world in which persons exist. As he writes in *Self and Others*, 'we cannot give an undistorted account of "a person" without giving an account of his relations with others'. This principle yields one of the key ideas of Laingian psychiatry: that we require 'confirmation' from others, and that where others systematically disconfirm our worth and our nature as agents we can be destroyed. In this sense, a depersonalising psychiatric practice represents collusion with the patient's madness.

The relationship between psychiatrist and patient must be a personal one, centred on 'the original bond of I and You'. The model of detached observation imported from natural science is here misplaced. (We may recall at this point Macquarrie's remark that 'the ideal of detachment' can be a hindrance.) The goal is understanding, not explanation. Laing comments: 'I think it is clear that by "understanding" I do not mean a purely intellectual process. For understanding one might say love'. In order to understand, it is necessary to enlist 'all the powers of every aspect of ourselves'. Though such personal involvement must represent, from the viewpoint of 'scientific' psychiatry, a departure from rationality and objectivity, it is a procedure which can be fully justified in terms of the epistemology of John Macmurray, in which knowledge and rationality are not restricted to intellection. Indeed, from a Macmurrayan perspective, it is a 'scientific' psychiatry which is irrational and subjective, since it constitutes a failure to 'behave in terms of the nature of the object'.

Laing's main political work is *Reason and Violence*, a study of Sartre's *Critique de la Raison Dialectique*, co-written with D.G. Cooper and published in 1964. Critics have complained of the book's obscurity, but the personalist emphasis of Laing's early work can be clearly identified here too. The project is to achieve a mitigation of Marxism's determinist moment by allowing for the reality of individual freedom and intentionality. 'What contemporary Marxists forget is that the man who is alienated, mystified, reified, and so on, remains none the less a man.' Sartre is praised for tracing 'the life of a person to its own ultimate issue.' For, Laing writes, 'it is only through the discovery of a freedom, a choice of self functioning in the face of all determinations, conditioning, fatedness, that we can attain the comprehension of a person in his full reality'.[27]

On the evidence of a remarkable recent essay entitled 'What is the matter with mind?', Laing's thought is now taking on new emphases. If in the early work Laing is resisting the illegitimate extension of natural scientific paradigms to the study of persons, now there is a much fiercer hostility to the scientific outlook, and concern about its ethical consequences. Here Laing echoes ideas which are prominent in the work of other Scottish thinkers, such as Baillie, Paton and Macmurray, if in much more polemical tones, arguing that the triumph of a scientist approach to the world has led to a catastrophic neglect and disestimation of such areas of our experience as our sense of value and our consciousness of ethical obligation.

The main theme of the essay is that science excludes from its sphere of investigation much of our ordinary reality:

> We know that meaning, value, quality, love and hate, good and evil, beauty and ugliness, exist in some sort of way, which is not a number or quantity, or a thing. We know, therefore, that we, our existing selves, are immeasurable. Job's balances are not to be found in a physicist's laboratory. The natural scientist explicitly excludes that subjective morass, he leaves all that behind, he sheds all he can of it, before even embarking on his voyage of scientific discovery. [28]

Science debars value,

> love and hate, joy and sorrow, misery and happiness, pleasure and pain, right and wrong, purpose, meaning, hope, courage, despair, God, heaven and hell, grace, sin, salvation, damnation, enlightenment, wisdom, compassion, evil, envy, malice, generosity, camaraderie. . .

The list, it is worth noting, contains a surprising number of religious categories.

But the scientific perspective is not a primary, pure, neutral, value-free apprehension of reality. As Laing writes in *The Divided Self*, it is not neutral 'to see a smile as contractions of the circumoral muscles'. Science in fact transforms primary experience. It involves, in Laing's memorable phrase, a *de-realisation of reality*, through an ablation of ordinary experience, an exclusion and devalorisation of whole fields of human experience which are perceived, except from the scientific perspective, as real. Reality and objectivity are denied to all those phenomena present to consciousness which are not amenable to quantification and experimental control.

> All sensibility, all values, all quality, all feelings, all motives, all intentions, spirit, soul, consciousness, subjectivity: almost everything, in fact, which we ordinarily take to be real is de-realised, is stripped of its pretensions to reality.

The victory of the scientific way of seeing reality signals a profound cultural mutation. For where ethics is divorced from fact and value from knowledge, where the conviction that 'all our subjective values are objectively valueless' gains ground, we witness the undermining of human responsibility towards being.

It might be objected, against our placing of Laing, that the parallels between his thought and that of other recent Scottish theorists are more or less fortuitous (improbable though this would be), and that the influence of local cultural traditions has been overstated. In reply we would draw attention to two elements in Laing's biography.

Our argument receives confirmation, in the first place, from the fact that in the 1950s Laing was a member of a Glasgow discussion group which had a marked existentialist and personalist orientation, and which, indeed, included certain of the other figures we have referred to above.

This informal circle was sometimes called 'the Abenheimer group', also 'the Schorstein group', after its two Jewish members who had emigrated to Glasgow—Karl Abenheimer and Joe Schorstein. Ronald Gregor Smith, the theologian, appears to have been a guiding intellectual presence in the group, which went into decline after his death in 1968. John Macquarrie, like Laing a former student at C.A. Campbell's Glasgow philosophy department, was another member. A very significant proportion of the group's membership, in fact, were theologians or churchmen.

Gregor Smith had little patience with analytic philosophy, and it was Continental thought which dominated the group's meetings. Thinkers discussed included Kierkegaard, Heideggor, Jaspers, Buber, Bultmann, Tillich, Sartre and Unamuno. Laing was a participant before moving to London, and read to the group drafts of *The Divided Self*.

Of the circle's intellectual ethos, Jack Rillie, another participant, has written that existentialist theology was one of the cohesive forces. 'Baillie, Macmurray, Buber,' he writes, 'were all in the conversational stream.' While acknowledging that not all members would have been happy to be termed 'personalists', Rillie observes that 'the predominant existentialist interest of the members certainly inclined it in that direction.'[29]

A second feature of Laing's biography, concerning his early life, also deserves emphasis. Like many of the other Scottish thinkers referred to here, Laing enjoyed what would now be called a 'strict' religious upbringing. In a *Listener* essay published in 1970, Laing wrote of this in the following way:

> I grew up, theologically speaking, in the nineteenth century: lower-middle-class Lowland Presbyterian, corroded by nineteenth-century materialism, scientific rationalism and humanism. . .I remember vividly how startled I was to meet for the first time, when I was eighteen, people of my age who had never opened a Bible. . . For the first time in my life, I could see myself being looked at rather as I imagine a native may see himself looked at by an attentive, respectful anthropologist. I could see myself regarded with incredulity by

an eighteen-year-old French girl, a student from the Sorbonne, as some idealistic barbarian still occupied by issues of religious belief, disbelief or doubt, still living before the Enlightenment, exhibiting in frayed but still recognisable form the primitive thought forms of the savage mind.[30]

If these words hint at a resolution of the conflict between 'Lowland presbyterianism' and secular rationalism in favour of the latter, and an approximation to the worldview of the girl from the Sorbonne, Laing's more recent work, as we have seen, with its appreciation of the significance of religious categories, suggests a rather different balance of forces. What is clear, in any case, is the tension between religious culture and *Aufklärung*, a contradiction which made acceptance of any purely scientific and secular philosophy impossible.

Laing's roots in a strongly moral-religious milieu should thus be seen as a key to his intellectual trajectory. This background — as in the case of other recent Scottish theorists — explains the inclination to question the claims of science, the concern with the threat posed to ethics by the spread of positivist modes of thought, and the refusal to ignore or disesteem the dimensions of experience, knowledge and reality which are beyond the scope of scientific reasoning.

In 1966, in the preface to the Pelican edition of *The Divided Self*, Laing wrote: 'If I am older, I am now also younger'. It is possible that he could today repeat those words with a different investment of meaning, given the emphasis of his recent work, in acknowledgement of the values he learned in his youth. Perhaps we could say of Laing's thought, too, as Walter Kaufmann has written of Buber's, that its problematic can be defined, ultimately, by the question: 'what does the religion of my fathers mean to me today?'

Conclusion

English culture, or to be more precise, the public-school, Oxbridge, 'Home Counties' formation is steeped, to a singular degree, in the bizarre belief that its own history, institutions and practices are paradigms for other less favoured peoples. It is therefore not surprising that when anglican chaps turn their attention to Scotland, their representations should reflect these assumptions of superiority: a violent history, a fanatical religion, an impoverished culture, a 'dark', 'backward', even 'uncivilised' country.

What is at first sight surprising is the fact that these images of backwardness and inferiority also govern the Scottish intelligentsia's discourse on Scotland. The overwhelming tendency of this discourse is to portray Scotland as a country which can be exhaustively described in terms of poverty, philistinism, bigotry, repression — a land of no gods or heroes.

This phenomenon can only be explained by means of the concept of inferiorisation: the loss of self-belief and acceptance of the superiority of metropolitan mores engendered by the sustained and ubiquitous institutional and ideological pressures which are exerted by 'core' powers on their satellites. In replicating and enlarging the metropolitan images of native retardation, the Scottish intelligentsia has fulfilled the same historic function as the colonial évolués whose sad condition was analysed by Frantz Fanon.

Inferiorist assumptions are deeply ingrained, and there have been very few attempts in serious writing to encode the Scottish experience in ways which do not rely on them. In this context, the significance of George Davie's work deserves special emphasis.

By examining the traditionally central concerns of Scottish culture — education and theory — in an approach which owes nothing to the orthodoxies of historical and cultural analysis, Davie has laid the groundwork for a decolonised understanding of Scotland. Where the official, inferiorist view could see in the Scottish educational tradition only moth-eaten practices best discarded, Davie has reconstructed the educational values and the cogent philosophy of education which they attempted to articulate. Where official history has tended to see in nineteenth and twentieth century Scotland an intellectual void, in his writing on, among others, Ferrier, Robertson Smith and Anderson, Davie has brought to light a vigorous and exciting cultural scene.

The *chiens de garde* of metropolitan representations of Scotland are numerous, powerful and vocal. But it would be wrong to conclude on an overly pessimistic note. In the 1980s, there has been a growth of interest in Davie's revolutionary work and the possibility it reveals of constructing a comprehension of the Scottish identity which is free from the distancing and paralysing assumptions of inferiorism.

For this reason, in a very rapidly intensifying political and cultural struggle, we look forward to the formation of a sophisticated opposition to the intellectual discourses which underwrite Scotland's subordination. These essays are intended as a continuation to that now long overdue project.

References

Chapter 1

1. Frantz Fanon (1967) *The Wretched of the Earth* p. 190.
2. *ibid.* p. 169.
3. Hugh Trevor-Roper 'Scotching the Myths of Devolution' *The Times* 28 April 1976
4. Fanon *op.cit.* p. 190.
5. *ibid.* p. 169.
6. Hugh Trevor-Roper (1967) 'The Scottish Enlightenment' *Studies on Voltaire and the 18th Century* p. 1636
7. Trevor-Roper 'Scotching the Myths . . . '
8. James D Young (1979) *The Rousing of the Scottish Working Class*
9. Andrew Cruikshank, (1977) *Scottish Bedside Book*, p. 162.
10. Tam Dalyell (1977) *Devolution: the End of Britain?* p. 281.
11. *ibid.* p. 283.
12. *ibid.* p. 282.
13. H.T. Buckle (1882) *History of Civilisation in England* Vol.3 p. 410.
14. Anne Smith 'Blow-out' *New Statesman* 10 September 1982
15. P.H. Scott 'Scotch Myths' *Bulletin of Scottish Politics* Vol. 1 No 2 Spring 1981 p. 65.
16. James D. Young (1979) *The Rousing of the Scottish Working Class*; and 'The Making of the Inarticulate Scot' *The Scotsman* 12 February 1977
17. T.C. Smout 'The Scottish Identity' in Robert Underwood (ed) (1977) *The Future of Scotland* p. 19.
18. W. Labov 'The Logic of Nonstandard English' partly reprinted in Pier Paolo Giglioli (ed) (1972) *Language and Social Context*
19. Tom Nairn (1977) *The Break-Up of Britain* pp. 162–3
20. *ibid.* p. 162.
21. Lindsay Paterson 'Scotch Myths' *Bulletin of Scottish Politics* Vol 1, No.2 Spring 1981.
22. Colin McArthur 'Breaking the Signs: 'Scotch Myths' as Cultural Struggle' *Cencrastus* No. 7 Winter 1981-82.
23. P.H. Scott *op.cit.*

Chapter 2

1. Frantz Fanon (1967) *The Wretched of the Earth.*
2. H.G. Graham (1909) *The Social Life of Scotland in the Eighteenth Century* p. X.
3. P. Hume Brown (1891) *Early Travellers in Scotland.*
4. H.R. Trevor-Roper 'The Scottish Enlightenment' *Studies on Voltaire and the Eighteenth Century* (1967) Vol. 58 pp. 1635–1658.
5 H.T. Buckle,(1970) *On Scotland and the Scotch Intellect* p. 207.
6. *ibid.* p. 225.
7. *ibid.* p. 171.
8. *ibid.* p. 384-6.
9. H. Hamilton (1932; Reprinted 1966) *The Industrial Revolution in Scotland*, Preface.
10. *ibid.* p. 3.
11. A.C. Chitnis (1976) *The Scottish Enlightenment* p. 44; see also pp. 251-4
12. R.H. Campbell (1965) *Scotland Since 1707. The Rise of an Industrial Society* p. 3.
13. Tom Nairn (1981) *The Break-Up of Britain* p. 140 our italics.
14. A.J. Youngson (1966) *The Making of Classical Edinburgh* Preface.
15. J.D. Hoeveler (1981) *James McCosh and the Scottish Intellectual Tradition*, p. 14 our italics.
16. *ibid.* p. 9.
17. Charles Camic,(1983) *Experience and Enlightenment: Socialisation for Cultural Change in Eighteenth Century Scotland.*
18. T.C. Smout (1969) *A History of the Scottish People* p. 145.
19. *ibid.* p. 170.
20. *ibid.* p. 225.
21. *ibid.* p. 227 our italics.
22. N.T. Phillippson and R. Mitchison (eds) (1970) *Scotland in the Age of Improvement* p. 1 our italics.
23. *ibid.* our italics.
24. *ibid.*
25. J.N. Wolfe (ed) (1969) *Government and Nationalism in Scotland* p. 200.

Chapter 3

1. H.G. Graham (1909) *The Social Life of Scotland in the Eighteenth Century* pp. 2-5.
2. *ibid.* p. 152; See also p. 169.
3. *ibid.* p. 152.
4. *ibid.* p. 153.
5. *ibid.* p. 79.
6. *ibid.* p. 178.
7. *ibid.* p. 166, our italics.
8. *ibid.* p. 166.
9. H. Hamilton (1932. Reprinted 1966) *The Industrial Revolution in Scotland* p. 5.

10. H. Hamilton (1963) *An Economic History of Scotland in the Eighteenth Century* p. 51.
11. Ian Whyte (1979) *Agriculture and Society in Eighteenth Century Scotland* p. 2.
12. J.A. Symon (1959) *Scottish Farming Past and Present.*
13. *ibid.* p. 102-3.
14. *ibid.* p. 106-7.
15. T.B. Franklin (1952) *A History of Scottish Farming*, p. 114.
16. *ibid.* p. 115.
17. J.E. Handley (1953) *Scottish Farming in the Eighteenth Century* p. 12.
18. *ibid.* quoted p. 14.
19. T.C. Smout (1972) *A History of the Scottish People 1560-1830* p. 141.
20. *ibid.* p. 125.
21. J.A. Symon *op.cit.* p. 141.
22. *ibid.* pp. 105-6.
23. *ibid.* p. 109.
24. J.B. Caird 'The Making of the Scottish Rural Landscape' in *Scottish Geographical Magazine* Vol. 80 (1964) p. 72.
25. I.M.M. MacPhail (1956) *A History of Scotland for Schools* Book II p. 11
26. *ibid.* quoted p. 19. For further illustration of the insinuation of the professional historians' views into school texts, see J Patrick (1972) *Scotland. The Age of Achievement.*
27. J.H.G. Lebon 'The Process of Enclosure in the Western Lowlands' *Scottish Geographical Magazine* Vol. 62 (1946) p. 104.
28. Alexander Fenton 'Scottish Agriculture and the Union: An Example of Indigenous Development' in T.I. Rae (ed) (1974) *The Union of 1707* p. 90.
29. I.D. Whyte *op.cit.* p. 4.
30. *ibid.* p. 2.
31. *ibid.* p. 199.
32. T.C. Smout *op.cit* p. 114.
33. I.D. Whyte *op.cit* p. 217
34. *ibid.* p. 255, our italics
35. D. Turnock (1982) *The Historical Geography of Scotland since 1707* p. 30.
36. *ibid.*

Chapter 4

1. Tom Nairn 'Internationalism: a critique' *Bulletin of Scottish Politics* Vol. 1 no. 1 Autumn 1980.
2. Tom Nairn 'Anatomy of the Labour Party' *New Left Review* Nos. 27 and 28 1964; and (1973) *The Left against Europe?.*
3. R. Balfe et al. 'Why we say no to the EEC' *New Statesman* 12 March 1982.
4. D.A. McIver 'Instant Memorial' (review of Drucker and Brown *The Politics of Nationalism and Devolution*) *Bulletin of Scottish Politics* Vol 1 No. 1 Autumn 1980.

5. Isaac Deutscher; quoted in Nairn *The Left against Europe?* p. 122.
6. Leszek Kolakowski (1981) *Main Currents of Marxism* Vol. 1 p. 417.
7. Tom Nairn (1981) *The Break-Up of Britain.*
8. Tom Nairn 'What really happened in Scotland' March 9, 1979, *New Statesman.*
9. Tom Nairn 'Dr Jekyll's Case: Model or Warning?' *Bulletin of Scottish Politics* Vol. 1 No. 1 Autumn 1980.
10. Colin McArthur (ed) (1982) *Scotch Reels: Scotland in Cinema and Television.* Quotation from editor's introduction.
11. Dennis Lee 'Country, Cadence, Silence', *Cencrastus* No. 4, 1981.
12. William Ferguson, 'The Origins and Nature of the Scottish Enlightenment', *Cencrastus* No. 11 New Year 1983.

Chapter 5

1. SNP Manifesto.
2. 'Conversation with A J Ayer' in Bryan Magee (ed) (1971) *Modern British Philosophy* p. 49.
3. *ibid.* p. 64.
4. *ibid.* p. 62.
5. R.C. Cross and A.D. Woozley (1964)*Plato's Republic: A Philosophical Commentary* p. 166.
6. Ernest Gellner (1968) *Words and Things* p. 41.
7. Quoted in Gellner *op.cit.* p. 111.
8. Ludwig Wittgenstein *Philosophical Investigations* p. 49 and p. 47.
9. Herbert Marcuse (1972) *One-Dimensional Man* p. 140.
10. 'The Philosophies of Moore and Austin: Conversation with Geoffrey Warnock' in Magee *op.cit.* p. 98.
11. Martin Walker 'Minds of Our Own' *The Guardian* January 9-11 1984.
12. Ludwig Wittgenstein, *Tractatus Logico-Philosophicus*, London, 1922, 6.53.
13. C.A. Campbell, *On Selfhood and Godhood*, London, 1957, pp. 36-7.
14. T.M. Knox, 'Two Conceptions of Philosophy', in *Philosophy*, Vol XXXVI, No. 138, October 1961, pp. 289–308.
15. H.J. Paton (1959) *The Modern Predicament* p. 377.
16. *ibid.*, p. 386.
17. H.J. Paton (1958) *The Categorical Imperative*, p. 17.
18. John Macmurray (1961) *Persons in Relation*, p. 224.
19. John Macmurray (1932) *Freedom in the Modern World*, p. 101.
20. John Baillie (1962) *The Sense of the Presence of God*, p. 253.
21. John Macquarrie (1973) *Existentialism*, 2nd edn., p. 221.
22. Alasdair MacIntyre (1988) *Whose Justice? Which Rationality?.* p.x.
23. Alasdair MacIntyre,(1971) *Marxism and Christianity.* p.106.

Chapter 6

1. George Davie (1961; Reprinted 1986) *The Democratic Intellect* p. 8.
2. *ibid.* p. 79.

3. *ibid*. p. 79.
4. *ibid*. p. 80.
5. *ibid*. p. 4.
6. *ibid*. p. 7.
7. *ibid*. p. 13.
8. *ibid*. p. 5.
9. *ibid*. p. 17.
10. *ibid*. pp. 23-4.
11. *ibid*. p. 235.
12. *ibid*. p. 28.
13. *ibid*. p. 32.
14. *ibid*. p. 59.
15. *ibid*. p. 61.
16. *ibid*. p. 49.
17. *ibid*. p. 67.
18. George Davie, 'John Anderson in Scotland', *Quadrant*, (Sydney), July 1977.
19. George Davie *The Crisis of the Democratic Intellect*, p. 61.
20. Eugene Kamenka, 'Anderson on Education and Academic Freedom', in John Anderson (1980) *Education and Inquiry*, (Ed. D.Z. Phillips), Blackwell, p. 32.
21. Anderson, op. cit., p. 130.
22. *ibid*. p. 72 (emphasis in original).
23. J. Mackie, 'Anderson's Theory of Education', in Anderson, op. cit., p. 16.
24. Anderson, op. cit., p. 99.
25. *ibid*., p. 43.
26. Ronald Santangeli, 'Back to Latin', *Times Educational Supplement* (Scotland), 11 November, 1983.
27. Anderson, op. cit., p. 107.
28. *ibid*. , p. 96.
29. *ibid*., p. 207.
30. On these points, see Geoffrey Partington, 'The Disorientation of Western Education', *Encounter*, January 1987.
31. BBC 1 Scotland, 1987.
32. On this point see for example Frank Palmer, 'Skillsology versus Culture', *The Use of English*, 38, 1, Autumn 1986, pp. 37–44.
33. Kamenka, *op. cit.*, p. 38.

Chapter 7

1. See for example H.R. Mackintosh (1937) *Types of Modern Theology*; Ian Henderson (1965) *Rudolf Bultmann*; Ronald Gregor Smith (1966) *Martin Buber*; T.F.Torrance (1962) *Karl Barth*; John Macquarrie (1955) *An Existentialist Theology*; (1968) *Martin Heidegger*.
2. See Craig Beveridge and Ronald Turnbull, 'John Anderson, Philosopher', *Cencrastus* (No. 19, Winter 1984), Robert Calder, 'The Heraklitean John Anderson', *Edinburgh Review*, August 1986;

and George Davie, *The Crisis of the Democratic Intellect*, Edinburgh, 1986.

3. Eugene Kamenka, 'Anderson on Education and Academic Freedom', in John Anderson, *Education and Inquiry*, (1980) D.Z. Phillips (ed) p. 20.
4. D.M. Armstrong, 'Self-Profile', in Radu J. Bogdan (ed) (1984) *D.M. Armstrong*, p. 7.
5. George Davie (1986) *The Crisis of the Democratic Intellect*, p. 50.
6. See for example 'The Servile State', reprinted in John Anderson (1962) *Studies in Empirical Philosophy*.
7. John Macquarrie (1982) *In Search of Humanity*, p. 69.
8. John Baillie (1962) *The Sense of the Presence of God*, p. 28.
9. John Macmurray (1969 edn.) *The Self as Agent*, p. 30.
10. *ibid*, p. 202.
11. Ronald Gregor Smith, translator's introduction to Martin Buber (1961) *Between Man and Man*.
12. Alasdair MacIntyre, 'Moral Rationality, Tradition, and Aristotle', *Inquiry*, Vol 26, 1983, p. 466.
13. Alasdair MacIntyre (1981) *After Virtue: a Study in Moral Theory*, p. 2.
14. Fred Inglis (1982) *Radical Earnestness: English Social Theory 1880–1980*.
15. MacIntyre, op. cit., p. 22.
16. *ibid.*, p. 262.
17. Alasdair MacIntyre (1970) *Marcuse*, p. 7.
18. Alasdair MacIntyre, *After Virtue*, p. 33.
19. *ibid.*, pp. 220-221.
20. *ibid.*, p. 34.
21. *ibid.*, p. 34.
22. *ibid.*, p. 118.
23. J. Richard Boston, 'The Divided Self', *The Guardian*, 3 August, 1976.
24. Alan Bold (1983) *Modern Scottish Literature*, Introduction.
25. George Davie, op.cit., p. 176.
26. R.D. Laing (1965) *The Divided Self*, p. 23.
27. R.D. Laing and D.G. Cooper (1971, 2nd ed) *Reason and Violence*, pp. 24-5.
28. R.D. Laing, 'What is the matter with mind?', in (1980) *The Schumacher Lectures*, Satish Kumar (ed), pp. 6-7.
29. Personal communication. This has now been published: Jack Rillie, 'The Abenheimer/Schorstein Group', *Edinburgh Review*, August–November 1987, pp. 104-107.
30. R.D. Laing, 'Religious Sensibility', *The Listener*, 23 April, 1970.

Index